Perfect
Harmony
The New Seekers Story

CW00551932

Neil Saint

NEW HAVEN PUBLISHING LTD

Published 2022
First Edition
NEW HAVEN PUBLISHING LTD
www.newhavenpublishingltd.com
newhavenpublishing@gmail.com

Front cover image © Barry Plummer Photographer

Cover Design © Pete Cunliffe

Contents

Contributors

Chris Barrington – Original member of the first New Seekers line up, staying with the group from 1969 to 1970.

Nic Culverwell – Manager of The New Seekers from 2003.

Brian Engle – A New Seeker directly after Danny Finn left for a short time in that late 70s/early 80s period, and the co-writer of their last single release to date.

Mick Flinn – A fellow Australian who knew Marty Kristian and Peter Doyle from their early days in music, a member of Springfield Revival from 1972 to 1975, a group who were stablemates of The New Seekers, and a New Seeker from 1981 onwards.

Eve Graham – A New Seeker from 1969 to 1974 and from 1976 to 1978. Eve was the lead vocalist on many of the group's most popular songs.

Sally Graham - As with Chris Barrington, an original member of The New Seekers' line up from 1969 to the summer of 1970.

Donna Jones – vocalist, with Lyn Paul, in the Chrys Do Lyns, a member of Springfield Revival from 1972-1975, and a New Seeker from 1980 onwards.

Marty Kristian – A New Seeker from 1969 to 1974 and from 1976 to 2002.

Paul Layton – The longest serving New Seeker, who was a key member of the group from 1970 to 1974 and from 1976 onwards.

David Mackay – The New Seekers' producer from 1970 to 1973, who was instrumental in those vocal arrangements which led to that distinctive group sound in their 'golden period' from 1970 to 1973.

Keith Potger – A key member of hit 60s group The Seekers and co-founder of The New Seekers with David Joseph. It was his idea to establish a separate group called The New Seekers.

Foreword

This book is a project conceived and written by Neil Saint with great energy and attention to detail. He has conscientiously followed the chronology of the various line ups of the group, intermixing this story with accounts and anecdotes from most of the past and present members but at the same time not forgetting those who are no longer with us, who I would like to mention and pay tribute to, namely: Peter Doyle, Kathy Ann Rae and Danny Finn.

Paul Layton

Introduction

Perfect Harmony: The New Seekers Story

The title implies, particularly as it is the first book to be published on the group in question, that this might be the definitive story of The New Seekers. Well, it is and it isn't, depending on an individual perspective.

For a start, on one level, for me The New Seekers can only be Paul Layton, Peter Doyle, Eve Graham, Marty Kristian and Lyn Paul, what I term the mark two line up. Whenever I think of the sound and image of The New Seekers I think of that 'golden era' line up, hence that cover photograph for the book.

Whilst I was fortunate and privileged to get three of the four surviving members of the group onside, unfortunately I wasn't able to get Lyn over the line with the project. Just to be clear, I have spoken to Lyn and I like to think, in the context of being a fan, I still maintain a warm relationship with her. However, it was agreed I would not use any of her words from my recording of our conversation together, a line I have stuck to with the material in the book.

On the other hand, Eve, in her communication with me, has been very encouraging, as has Marty, and Paul, who I see, being the longest serving member of the group, as the curator of The New Seekers legacy (and rightly so in my opinion). To reassure you, material from the conversations I shared with Eve, Marty and Paul form a strong core of the book.

Peter Doyle, who is no longer with us, is fondly remembered throughout the book and as Mick Flinn states he is undoubtedly 'one of Australia's best ever singers'. With Peter Doyle leaving the group you could say the 'perfect harmony' of The New Seekers stopped at that point; but then again, with a new member, Larry, becoming a new Peter (this time Oliver not Doyle), with that change The New Seekers continued... although of course they were never to sound the same as the mark two line up. As you may know, after that mark three incarnation, with Larry Oliver involved, the brand stopped for a while, in 1974, although after that they re-ignited in 1976, continuing well into the new millennium.

Turning to The New Seekers' family tree, for me Paul Layton sits at the top below god. And who is god you may ask? Well there are two gods in my opinion and they are both Australian! David Joseph, who since 2012 is no longer with us, showing that underneath any 'tough businessman guise' David was most certainly human, and the musical legend Keith Potger, who alongside David came up with the idea of an entirely separate group flying the flag for The Seekers. However, with two female singers this time around it would be a 'new' Seekers group with a very different sound, yet together they would produce vocals that would nevertheless be 'in perfect harmony'. In co-creating The New Seekers surely Keith can be conferred god-like status?

It's strange such strong Australian DNA runs through the veins of a group that many viewed as being 'very British', who, with the amount of time they spent singing on their programmes, almost seemed to be endorsed by the BBC. Peter Doyle was Australian born and Marty mostly identifies as being Australian, although at the same time he recognises his international pedigree. Alongside them, Australian Mick Flinn, as you will read, played a very significant role in The New Seekers' story early on in Australia, during those days of success in the UK and later on, too, as the hits had stopped coming. With arguably five Australians connected with the group, the Australian link appropriately continues with myself as the group's story teller, having joint British/Australian citizenship. As Marty will tell you, as a cynic turned believer after visiting Mrs Knowles (and you can read about that in the book), 'some things were just meant to be'. It's strange to think my earliest notion of any real Australia came from watching *Skippy The Bush Kangaroo* on TV.

Whilst it may not be 'definitive', 'authorised 'or 'official', on the other hand this is more than just the story of The New Seekers as it is also and at the same time, from a 21st century information superhighway perspective, the story of the long gone radio and TV age, when no internet existed and music (and hits in the charts) ruled the entertainment world in Britain. Music quite simply was there all around us, breathed in like oxygen.

The story begins when the sounds of early Elvis greeted a young Eve Graham, when she heard him sing 'Heartbreak Hotel' on that jukebox in Perth, Scotland. She must have experienced a similar excitement as the young Marty Kristian when in Melbourne he pestered his mum to fund his first guitar. The television age was sleepily dawning as teenage music became a commercial entity in 1964; after the pirate radio stations offered a diet of the pop music that helped record labels sell 45s, *Top Of The Pops* was born at the BBC and later on Radio 1, where pop music was constantly played, with that most British of broadcasting companies offering on radio only a meagre diet of that music before then. Whilst in the 60s there were popular music TV shows such as *Ready Steady Go* in the UK and *The Go! Show*, *Kommotion* and *Bandstand* in Australia, for me the onset of the TV age began with the onset of colour TV. It's hard to imagine that groundbreaking BBC programmes such as *Dr Who* and *Top Of The Pops* to begin with were broadcast to viewers watching in black and white.

The New Seekers, unlike The Seekers, were a group that seem constructed for this coloured TV age, where the new values of having to look good on TV (in Marc Bolan's case with make-up and corkscrew hair) built on the old values that remained as variety entertainment continued. In looking good on TV, the mark two line up of The New Seekers demonstrated they could maintain that balancing act, with their performance in Edinburgh at the 1972 Eurovision Song Contest final a good example. Whilst many people would have been watching the contest in colour, the vast majority of families would have been renting their TV set. To give readers a flavour of this TV era I have included details throughout the book of some of the popular programmes that were broadcast. It is hard to imagine *Love Thy Neighbour* as anything but a crazy idea and it is shocking to think the older generation may have casually enjoyed *The Black & White Minstrel Show* without experiencing any sense of shame. Why else would that programme have continued to be broadcast until 1978?

Returning to the theme as to whether this is a definitive story of The New Seekers, well, of course, without Lyn's words it can't be; however, taking that line you could argue that without the words of all the twenty members it can't be either! Consequently this book represents the story of The New Seekers through the eyes of some of the key participants. Of course the words of those participants will only be their 21st century version of the truth, subject to error, embellishment and mis-remembering of facts. It is impossible for me to take the reader back in time and of course participants are remembering events that happened to them when they were young adults from the perspective of elderly people in their seventies. I make no apologies for the fact that an 'in their own words' tale through the eyes of participants can not ever be a story that contains definitive truth. However, the book is still an interesting read, and during the 2018-2022 period these key individuals told me their take on the unique and unusual events that happened to them some while ago.

As the author of this book I feel my role is not to explain, but to manage the material I gathered, and present what I see as 'the story'. However, with a book of this nature it is important to be clear on what to include, as well as what to leave out.

Whilst it was disappointing that Larry Oliver felt his role was not significant enough for me to speak with him, he does have a point, as he was only in The New Seekers for a very short period. I had no control over leaving his perspective out of the mix.

Instinctively I felt that the mark two era was the most important part of The New Seekers' story, yet after the group stopped altogether in 1974, with the Keith Potger/David Joseph involvement finishing then too, the brand actively continued from 1976 (with Eve coming back into the group, Danny Finn replacing Peter Oliver and Kathy Ann Rae replacing Lyn Paul) to 2010 (with several versions of the group established around Marty Kristian, up to 2002, and Paul Layton as the mainstays after Eve finally left). Consequently I was faced with the dilemma of whether I continued to tell the story of The New Seekers after the hits dried up (the last single that met with chart success was released in 1978) or not.

Discovering that the story of The New Seekers after the second departure of Eve was a rich one, I had to keep going - to the end (but maybe there will be still more to tell?). With that, as there were quite a few changes in personnel, I decided that as well as talking with Paul Layton and Marty Kristian (who stayed on until 2002) I had to include the stories from key 'later period 'personnel, which is the reason why the views of Brian Engel (a person already experienced in the music business who was part of that first post-Eve line up), Nic Culverwell (who managed the group's reboot from 2003 which drove them towards album chart success in 2009), Donna Jones and Mick Flinn (only Marty and Paul have been New Seekers longer than these two members of the group's family) have been included. As The New Seekers are best epitomised by that 1970-1973 mark two line up I decided not to delve any deeper than that, as I feared the latter day phase would have overshadowed the true legacy of the group. As a result I apologise to Vivien, Nicola, Catriona, Vikki, Francine and Mark, as they were all valued members of The New Seekers at some time or other during that 1978 to 2010 period.

Cathy (first of all Kathy Ann and then Kathy) Rae was a very special person but unfortunately as she is no longer with us it would have been impossible to have spoken with her. I'm afraid Kevin (known as Danny) Finn, who was a member of The New Seekers from 1976 to 1978, has also died.

Equally irresistible not to include was the backstory of the group before they came into existence and a focus on the mark one line up. Thanks go to Nic Culverwell for hooking me up with Chris Barrington, who as a member of that line up left (to be replaced by Paul Layton from his old school), alongside Sally Graham and Laurie Heath, who in butting heads with David Joseph one time must have had quite a strong personality as a teenager! Chris and Sally told me first hand the reasons behind their departures, and their reasons differed slightly from what others had thought!

On top of this I felt it was also important to include Mick Flinn and Donna Jones's history before joining the group, as what they had to say was so deeply entwined with the early days of The New Seekers, most especially as Springfield Revival, the group they were in with Ray Martin, was on the roster that Keith Potger and David Joseph managed. Furthermore there is a strong argument that as Keith's interest waned in The New Seekers, ironically around the time they experienced New Seekermania in 1972 after Eurovision, his interest in a folk alternative through Springfield Revival increased. Also it is possible that with David Joseph being based in the US he may have taken his eye off the ball with The New Seekers as he looked to break this new project in that huge country, partially succeeding when he gained a spot for them to play in LA alongside a young Michael Jackson at the 1973 Oscar ceremony. Surely these details can't be left out? Maybe Peter Doyle could and should have stayed in the group? An enticing 'what if' thought...

In terms of what I chose to leave out, this is not a book where you will find details on every live gig the group played at or every TV programme they appeared on; nevertheless I did look to represent what I believe were the key moments in the group's history (I submit another apology to people who feel I may have got this wrong) and at least present a fan's perspective in the overviews of album releases. Effectively I have tried to tell the story of The New Seekers without including every little detail, which of course is impossible. As this is a book for fans of the group, I hope at least with the spirit of the book I have left nothing too important behind.

The sound of The New Seekers at their peak was special. Aside from the group harmonising, who created their sound? Keith Potger certainly got the ball rolling in coaching those first two versions of The New Seekers to sing those perfect harmonies. However, known to be behind many Australian hits, first of all working for EMI in the UK and then breaking away to become an independent producer, you might say David Mackay was The New Seekers' version of George Martin in producing them (though Michael Lloyd did a fine job too). You could say that rather like the fifth Beatle, David Mackay was in fact the sixth New Seeker. Having spoken to him, with some of the details from that interview of course included in this book, I can definitely vouch for him being a great guy, as can (and do) Eve, Keith, Marty, Paul and Mick. Why was he so special? Well, he was a genuine lover of music, a gifted musician and someone who always tried to make every release he produced special and unique. I won't tell you here how he did that with The New Seekers' first hit, as his account is there in the book for you to read and enjoy! Suffice to say there were many components that went into the mix in creating the perfect harmony of The New Seekers. If you'd permit me, let me tell you the story...

Neil Saint
January 2022

Introducing The New Seekers From The Golden Era

Eve Graham
I was born Evelyn May Beatson in 1943 Auchterarder.

In all honesty I would say I experienced a pretty normal childhood living there. Being in Scotland we heard rock 'n' roll on the radio but to us at that time that world seemed a million miles away from the place where we all lived.

It never ever occurred to me I'd make a career as a singer when I was younger.

Peter Doyle passed away in 2001 and was born on the 28th July 1949 in Abbotsford, an inner city suburb of Melbourne.

Backed by The Phantoms, in Australia he released ten singles between 1965 and 1967. In 1968 he joined The Virgil Brothers, Australia's answer to The Walker Brothers, with the single 'Temptation 'Bout To Get Me 'even becoming a top five hit there. The group relocated to the UK by the time of their third single, produced by David McKay, with Peter leaving the trio soon afterwards and of course then joining the second line up of The New Seekers.

Lyn Paul was born Lynda Belcher in 1949 Wythenshawe, a suburb of Manchester.

Although her parents were music lovers they didn't work in the entertainment industry. At the age of 14 she formed a singing group called the Chrys Do Lyns, referencing each girl's name, with two friends from the Joan Lawrence Dancing School, which she attended away from school.

One of those friends was Donna Jones, who was later to become part of The New Seekers after Lyn left, whilst the other singer was Christine Lowe, who was later to run The New Seekers fan club using the name Jill Webster.

At 17 she successfully auditioned for Manchester-based group The Nocturnes, singing alongside Eve Graham.

Marty Kristian
I was born Martin Vanags in 1945 Leipzig to Latvian parents but my name is now officially Martin Kristian. My family immigrated to Melbourne, Australia in 1950.

Whilst I have lived for a long while in the UK and I was born in Germany I still have a strong affiliation with Australia, experiencing my schooling and developing my strong interest in music there.

Having already performed on TV in Australia I came over to the UK working my passage by duetting with my friend Colin Cook on a ship called The Fairstar. Making a connection with Ken Pitt, I moved into accommodation that was previously lived in by David Bowie.

Knowing me from my TV work in Australia, David Joseph tracked me down and sold The New Seekers to me as a project.

Paul Layton

I was born in 1947 Beaconsfield, Buckinghamshire, although my family soon moved to Harrow in Middlesex.

There I experienced a very warm and loving lower middle class upbringing. My father, a German Jew, had moved over to the UK just before the war, where he met and romanced my mother, an English Jew. I was brought up in a non orthodox but progressive Jewish community.

With a strong interest in drama, I enrolled in The Ada Foster Theatre School in Golders Green, North West London.

Students there were mostly girls looking to become dancers, whereas the boys were looked upon as a commercial entity and sent to more auditions than the girls. Unfortunately we had the bad fortune of having to wear pink blazers and sometimes got ribbed about this on the school bus.

My father bought me my first guitar. Strumming along on that I eventually became able to write some three chord songs.

Before joining The New Seekers I was successful in gaining a recording contract with cool US label Elektra, home of The Doors, ironically the label the group also signed with later on!

The Golden Era Line Up

From the summer of 1970 to Peter Doyle's leaving in June 1973 this mark two line up had nine UK hit singles, which included their first number one,' I'd Like To Teach The World To Sing (In Perfect Harmony)'.

The New Seekers are from left to right Paul Layton, Eve Graham, Marty Kristian, Peter Doyle and Lyn Paul.

'It was really the combination of those five voices that made The New Seekers one of the best groups in the UK. That line up blew me away, they were just fantastic!' Mick Flinn

Chapter 1
Searching Out Something New: Elvis in '58 To The Seekers Disbanding In '68

30th January 1958 – The single 'Jailhouse Rock' by Elvis Presley enters the UK chart at number 1

EVE GRAHAM (vocalist in The New Seekers from 1969 to 1974 and from 1976 to 1978): My first memory of hearing pop music was listening to Radio Luxembourg under my bed covers.

When I was about 15 or so we used to go to the cafés in Perth, where we played records on the jukebox. In those days I wasn't old enough to buy records. That's where I first heard Elvis.

Coming from Scotland you went two ways: you either went in a very traditional Scottish direction wearing tartan or you followed the rock 'n' roll scene.

As we got older and left school some of the guys bought motorbikes. The usual thing was to have your hair slicked back and wear leather jackets. To me I had this 'if you can't beat 'em join 'em' attitude. As I couldn't stand how the girls stood around these guys giggling to attract their attention, with a friend we got motorbikes and became part of the gang.

5th February 1959 – The single 'To Know Him Is To Love Him' by The Teddy Bears reaches a peak position of number 2 in the UK charts

EVE GRAHAM: My dad used to sing Gilbert & Sullivan at concert parties. I did a little bit of that myself when I was about 15 or so. After that, with two school friends from Perth Academy, we'd sing along in harmony to the songs we would hear on the radio. At one point we became a small act in my dad's concert party, which was the first time I sang on stage. We were called The Short Cuts and for instance I remember we sang The Teddy Bears hit 'To Know Him Is To Love Him'.

I don't remember being scared when I sang in front of an audience for the first time. I actually don't think you're nervous when you're young. It is only later on when the nerves come in, when you wonder if you'll make a mistake. Back then it was just fun and we enjoyed it.

15

There were no nerves involved, for us it was just an adventure.

21st May 1959 – Marty Kristian persuades his mum to buy him a guitar on his 14th birthday from a Melbourne musical instrument shop called The Banjo Club

MARTY KRISTIAN (vocalist in The New Seekers from 1969 to 1974 and from 1976 to 2002): I was always musical. In fact I could knock out a tune supposedly on the harmonica before I was three years old.

Mum tried to push me in the direction of classical music and wanted me to take piano lessons. Someone gave her a violin that she wanted me to practise with but I had no interest in that at all.

As time went by, listening to the radio I enjoyed Elvis, Chuck Berry and Little Richard. I very much wanted to sing that style of songs.

Begging my mum to buy me a guitar, she bought me a Bellini on my birthday which I believe cost her two weeks' wages.

I was in raptures getting the guitar. I managed to learn three chords by going down to the local banjo club with about thirty or so others where I learnt to play my favourite rock 'n' roll songs.

5th July 1960 – The Elvis Presley single 'Mess of Blues' is released on RCA

Although initially released as the B side of 'It's Now or Never', it charts independently. Whilst it doesn't even reach the top 30 in the US it is a hit in Australia and is clearly a favourite of teenager Marty Kristian.

MARTY KRISTIAN: In an era where there was very little music on TV, when I was around 16 I entered a local talent show on the radio called *The Three Gong Award*. There were all sorts of people that went on this show. For instance Olivia Newton John went on it and won.

Packing my guitar up on a Saturday morning and going to the studios on a tram, I arrived to discover performers were faced with three judges on one side with a lady pianist I know now as Mabel Nelson, who accompanied the great Australian classical vocalist Dame Joan Sutherland, on the other. The challenge was to make it to the end of your performance (for the 'Three Gongs'). A gong before that signified you had to stop. When it was my turn I launched into 'Mess Of Blues' by Elvis, which I had learnt. However in my excitement I dislodged my guitar strap so the instrument started falling down to my knees. With there being no second chance with the programme going out live I had no choice but to plough on. Mabel noticed my predicament, grabbing my arms and supporting the guitar all the way through the rest of my performance. Later I was shocked to discover that not only had I managed to reach the end of the performance without a gong, I had also won the competition.

I had become a legend in my own school yard.

Once I left school, as I enjoyed drawing I studied architecture at Melbourne University. The first two years were fine, but when it got onto the serious mathematics, finding this difficult, I dropped out and continued singing. Carol West, who managed other singers, arranged for me to perform three songs on a programme called *Saturday Date in Sydney*. I had to fly up to Sydney and record songs to backtracks at a studio behind a butcher's shop owned by Ossie Byrne, who produced the early recordings of The Bee Gees. From there one thing led to another and I eventually performed regularly on Melbourne's *The Go!! Show* singing the hits of the day.

17th August 1960 – The Beatles' first performance in Germany takes place at The Indra Club in Hamburg

Whilst John, Paul and George are all present, it is Stuart Sutcliffe who is the bassist rather than Paul McCartney. There is no Ringo as Pete Best is the drummer.

EVE GRAHAM: After singing with The Short Cuts, I joined another Scottish group called The Cyclones. We played barn sized venues in the North and East of Scotland.

This all-male group had a pianist, drummer, bassist and guitarist. They didn't really want a female singer but they had to get one in order for them to tour Germany. I felt they viewed me as a little sister they had to drag around the playground. At that time the idea of performing in Germany was 'the thing to do' and we did this around the same time the earliest version of The Beatles performed there.

I remember travelling from Scotland to our first venue in Cologne in an old beat up van. The journey took forever.

1962 – The Seekers are formed from the embers of Australian doo wop group The Escorts

The first line up consists of school friends Athol Guy, Bruce Woodley and Keith Potger, with Ken Ray as lead singer. Ken Ray soon leaves the group to get married and is replaced by established jazz singer Judith Durham.

KEITH POTGER (A member of The Seekers, founder of The New Seekers and their co-manager with David Joseph from 1969 to 1974): After the breakup of The Escorts, Athol Guy and Bruce Woodley had got together to sing a few songs. With Ken Ray, lead singer in The Escorts, who had come back to Melbourne from Sydney with me, I joined forces with them.

One of the venues we were rehearsing at (and having a lot of fun at too) was this place in Toorak, an inner city suburb in Melbourne, owned by one of Athol Guy's best friends, which adjoined David Joseph's apartment. It was at one of those apartment blocks where everyone got together and had a good time.

At that time David was working at an advertising agency as a Creative Director, where he would have been involved in making creative decisions about music. The first musical connection I made with David was when he asked me to write jingles in the style of the current hit records for his advertising agency in Melbourne. The Seekers recorded the jingles about a year or so before the group left on our fortuitous journey to the UK. He had a very good sense about what might become successful as a commercial enterprise.

David ended up becoming more or less a lifelong friend as well as the co-manager of The New Seekers with me.

3rd March 1963 – The world premiere of the film *I Could Go On Singing* takes place in London

The film stars Judy Garland, Dirk Bogarde and Jack Klugman, an American perhaps still most famous for playing the Medical Examiner 'Quincey' on TV. Paul Layton has a small part in this film.

PAUL LAYTON (vocalist/bassist with The New Seekers from 1970 to 1974 and from 1976 onwards): Auditioning through school, I managed to gain a part in the Judy Garland film *I Could Go On Singing*. My parents were fans of Judy Garland and I was also particularly fond of the *Live At The Carnegie Hall* album. Although I didn't have a huge part in the film it was a very memorable experience as we sang songs around the piano with Judy in The Green Room.

I used to go to Baker Street in order to get on a minibus to Shepperton Studios at an unearthly hour. I remember Judy Garland's daughter Liza Minelli was also on that bus. At that time she had a romance with Greg

Phillips, who acted in the film, and attended The Italia Conti Academy of Theatre Arts.

Although The New Seekers toured with Liza later on I already knew her quite well.

In 1963 Manchester vocal group The Chrys Do Lyns (the 'Do' from Doreen - Donna's original name - is pronounced 'dough') is established, which consists of two future members of The New Seekers, Donna Jones and Lyn Paul, as well as the group's future fan club secretary Christine Lowe, who will use the name Jill Webster in this role.

DONNA JONES (vocalist with The New Seekers from 1980 onwards): I lived in Wythenshawe, several bus stops away from Lynda Belcher (who sang in The New Seekers as Lyn Paul from 1970 to 1974), as Lyn was known then. Although my parents had to work hard to make ends meet I was an only child growing up within a loving family. As with Lyn's situation, my parents were working class but at the same time they were very grounded people.

From the age of three I went to a dance school. My teacher Mr Cooper felt I had such potential that when my parents couldn't afford to pay for lessons any more he allowed me to attend lessons for free. Eventually I attended The Joan Lawrence Dance School, where I met Lyn and Christine.

After Lyn had seen an article in *Romeo* magazine which stated that there were no girl vocal groups around, she asked at one of our classes whether anybody would be interested in joining her in putting that sort of group together. From memory it was just Christine Lowe and I that turned up at Lyn's house. With the three of us forming the group from there we used to always rehearse at either Christine or Lyn's house.

Lyn's dad was the only parent out of the three families who had a car so, as much as he was able to, he would drive us to all these working men's clubs where we sang. He was a tremendous support and always very encouraging. The three of us got on really well. If Mr Belcher couldn't take us we'd all get on the bus with our costumes on. Christine would come over to my house, then we'd go to the bus stop near where I lived. We'd tell Lyn when we were going to meet her and five stops along the route she'd get on the bus with us in there already. We'd usually get a bus to the middle of Manchester and then take another from there to go wherever we were singing. Travelling was hard work as we couldn't afford a taxi.

We progressed from the working men's clubs in and around Manchester to performing at British army bases abroad, starving in France

19

and Germany, where we were even chaperoned by Joan Lawrence herself. I was 16, Christine was 15 and Lyn was just 14.

After my experience with the Chrys Do Lyns I only ever wanted to become a professional singer. I didn't think there was anything else I could do. Reflecting back it was tough but I didn't have any doubts about going in that direction as I loved it so much.

I eventually gained a residency singing at a nightclub called Mr Smiths in Manchester.

8th May 1963 – The Beatles hit the UK number 1 spot for the first time with the single 'From Me To You'

DONNA JONES: The Chrys Do Lyns sang all the old songs and gave them a modern slant.

As The Beatles, who we loved, had got going by that time I think we would have been much better singing the songs that were in the charts of the day.

There was never any thought about writing our own songs as coming from a dance school we were much more focused on performing.

EVE GRAHAM: In 1963 I felt like I was 20 going on 12.

I responded to a formal advert placed by a company called The Cyril Stapleton Orchestra Ltd. As leader of the BBC Show Band, Cyril had been a fixture on the English musical scene, broadcasting across the country throughout the mid-1950s, but by this point in time he had left the BBC and had his own group.

There was no way I would have had the confidence to have taken off on my own to look for work in London yet I was asked to go down there to audition. The audition was in front of Cyril Stapleton himself, who at that time was just a keyboard player.

It was a very daunting experience for me. I still have a vivid memory of walking into that dance hall for the first time with a polished floor and glitter ball spinning from the ceiling with all these wonderful coloured lights twirling around. I'd never seen anything like that before. I'd never even been to the dance halls in Glasgow. Maybe there was one like that there? I was totally taken aback by all of it.

I sang a couple of songs for him and Cyril asked me to come back in a week as I guess he clearly had a lot of auditions to get through. I was thrown by this. I had to tell him I didn't think I could stay that long as I didn't have enough money. He asked if I had a nice dress. I told him I did so I was asked to come back that evening wearing it. That evening Cyril told me to do the same as what I had done during the audition, which I did, but this time I performed in front of the whole orchestra. Afterwards he put me on a two week trial and gave me twenty pounds. Before I left I was earning five pounds a week so it was quite a hike in wages.

He found out that I hadn't organised anywhere to stay. Cyril ended up taking me to the digs in Streatham where the previous singer had been staying, driving me there in his Rolls Royce! I remember sitting in the car thinking this was all a bit posh for me.

It was thanks to his kindness I stayed, as without that I would have gone back to Scotland. I was totally out of my depth. My parents were naive about the whole thing too for letting me go. My dad just gave me twenty pounds. Later on I was able to phone my parents and put their minds at rest. I told them I had got a job and I was staying with a nice lady. They must have wondered whether they would ever see me again after seeing me off earlier in the day.

I did my two weeks trial and stayed on. Cyril was like a kind uncle, he was really great with me. I remember just before my twenty-first birthday going into his dressing room where there was a big pile of singles. He asked me to learn as much as I could. Luckily I was young and my mind was sharp so I could do that. Listening to records on a Dansette for instance I sang in front of the orchestra having learnt six songs for the first time that same night. Pop songs in those days were quite simple, two verses, a bridge, and normally the first verse all over again. I learnt them very quickly so I was able to build up a repertoire. That was how I got started.

When I first went down to London I performed at the Locarno, which was part of the Mecca group, where Cyril had a residency. All that summer I was working six nights a week as well as two afternoons. That was fine for me but apart from that I was sitting in my digs. I just went out on stage to perform then I went back to my digs. I was literally watching the clock, waiting to perform. I stayed in my room on my days off, which of course without knowing anyone was a bit lonely, but I had no desire to party. Naive isn't the word. I was just like a child being wheeled onto the stage, being wound up to sing and then coming off again ready to do that again!

I didn't perform to show others how good I was. In those days I wasn't really aware of the audience. At that time they were just dancing around the ballroom. For me it was the whole experience of singing with a big orchestra in such a great atmosphere with all those lights. It was a totally different world than I had ever been used to. I was just lapping all that up really. I was very suddenly dumped into this career and it was a big shock.

Cyril eventually left Mecca so then we travelled and performed at these private functions which were very lucrative. However, this meant I

21

had two days of work and five days sitting in my room. Even though it was a year further on I was just as naive and so I still didn't go out.

When I'm in front of ten thousand people I'm fantastic but when I'm not doing that I prefer to be on my own. However, it just got to be too lonely so I quit and returned home to Scotland.

I remember thinking I had a nice experience but that the whole thing had ended.

2nd November 1963 – Beatlemania is born!
With the word appearing as a headline in The Daily Mirror, it is the first time it is used in the media.

CHRIS BARRINGTON (a member of the first line up of The New Seekers from 1969 to 1970): Although I was born in 1950 Lancashire, situated in the North of England, my family moved to London when I was just two years old. My father thought I should lose my Northern accent (famously Beatles producer George Martin had taken elocution lessons to rid himself of his London accent) as in those days not having a regional accent presented you with more opportunities. Consequently I attended The Dorian English Stage School in the evenings to practise my speech, which was where I first met Laurie Heath (who also successfully auditioned for that first New Seekers line up).

The owner, Dorian English, sent students out to audition and when I was nine I acted in my first TV commercial, where I advertised Smarties [very popular British confectionery]. For some reason my acting resonated with directors so I made a whole slew of commercials. From a personal perspective I would say my childhood was fairly shabby, with my parents divorcing, and by the age of 12 I had retreated into my own world. I became completely self-sufficient from that age. When my father left the family home my mother was managing a shoe shop in Putney but not bringing in much money so my earnings were important. I was working pretty much every single day on TV commercials and radio broadcasts.

I eventually chose to attend The Ada Foster Theatre School because it had the best reputation out of the options that were available. Of course Laurie Heath and Paul Layton also attended the school. I paid to go there myself from the money I earned for my work in commercials. By that stage I was a successful jobbing actor. I wasn't ambitious; I just went with the flow. I enjoyed being picked up in a limousine every morning to be taken to an engagement at Pinewood Studios. It was fantastic, I loved that experience. I was simply having fun!

We had to wear pink blazers and I used to get beaten up so many times at the bus stop waiting to travel to school.

At Ada Foster I met a circle of friends that were keen on music so, with Beatlemania starting, I picked up the guitar.

23rd November – The first ever episode of *Dr Who* is shown on BBC1

It is broadcast by the BBC later than scheduled due to the station's coverage of JFK's assassination the previous day over-running.

As many of us will know, Dr Who *is based around the central humanoid alien character who used a Tardis, which had the appearance of a British police telephone box, as a vehicle for time travel. In those days before smart phones the police had special keys to use such boxes. The programme was originally intended to appeal to a family audience as an educational programme using time travel as a means to explore scientific ideas and famous moments in history.*

It has subsequently become a British TV phenomenon.

1st January 1964 – The first ever episode of *Top Of The Pops* is broadcast on BBC1

The programme becomes a British music TV behemoth with families gathering together 'in perfect harmony', if age and generation differences are put to one side, to watch the forty minute editions every early Thursday evening without fail.

At this moment in time it is only for black and white television. Tonight's first edition is hosted by radio disc jockeys Alan Freeman and Jimmy Savile. The debut studio performer is Dusty Springfield, singing her top 10 UK hit 'I Only Want To Be With You', a song later covered to great effect by British New Wave band The Tourists in the 80s with this time a fantastic vocal coming from their lead singer Annie Lennox. There are further studio appearances from The Rolling Stones with 'I Wanna Be Your Man', a song famously given to them by The Beatles, The Dave Clark Five with their hit 'Glad All Over', The Hollies performing 'Stay', The Swinging Blue Jeans singing 'Hippy, Hippy Shake' and Freddie & The Dreamers appearing with 'You Were Made For Me'. The Beatles song 'She Loves You' is played over the chart run down, a tradition that will continue on the show, whilst there is also a music video for their number one hit 'I Want To Hold Your Hand'.

Cliff Richard & The Shadows have been granted two music videos, one for their hit 'Don't Talk To Him' and another for a song not even released as a single.

The Gene Pitney classic '24 Hours From Tulsa' is played whilst there is a shot of the audience dancing. Dance groups interpreting a track for the watching audience became a tradition first with The Go Jos but later, perhaps most famously, with all-female group Pan's People.

Why has it become so popular and legendary? I guess because it never strays from the original format, concentrating on the best selling popular music in the UK with the artists that perform those singles highlighted on the show.

4th November 1964 – Australian group The Seekers record 'I'll Never Find Another You', written by Tom Springfield, at Abbey Road studios in London

The Seekers, formed in Melbourne, were offered a twelve month contract on the Sitmar Line passenger cruise ship Fairsky, which travelled to the UK in March 1964. Upon arrival they were offered work by a booking agency and began to appear regularly on a TV series hosted by Northern Irish singer Ronnie Carroll. Filling in on a bill headlined by British singer Dusty Springfield, they met her brother Tom Springfield. The single was released by EMI and championed by pirate radio station Radio Caroline. In February 1965 it reached the UK number one spot and became the seventh best selling single that year; however, later on the single 'The Carnival Is Over' eclipsed that commercial success, selling over a million units. Athol Guy, Bruce Woodley and Keith Potger provide musical accompaniment, as well as backing vocals, although the forlorn lead vocal of Judith Durham is the focal point.

This promotional photograph shows The Seekers from left to right at the front as Keith Potger, Judith Durham and Bruce Woodley with the double bass playing Athol Guy there at the back

EVE GRAHAM: After returning to Scotland I missed the whole buzz of London so in 1964 I went back down to Mecca where all my contacts were. At first I got a job as a catering manageress in Shaftesbury Avenue. I was told a new club was opening in Manchester and that they were auditioning for the group that was going to take up a residency there. I successfully auditioned in Blackpool and sang with The Nocturnes AKA Les Nocturnes at Tiffanys, on Oxford Street in Manchester. To start with I sang alongside Sandra Stevens, who later became a singer in The Brotherhood of Man.

KEITH POTGER: By the time The Seekers left for England, David Joseph had become quite successful.

He was running a radio station and was also managing singers in Australia, the most successful of which was Normie Rowe, who went on to have number one releases over there in the shape of double A sides 'Que Sera Sera'/'Shakin' All Over' in 1965 and 'Ooh La La'/'Ain't Nobody Home' in 1966.

For a while I lost contact with David, as he was over in Australia whilst I was based in the UK with The Seekers.

EVE GRAHAM: It wasn't my idea to use the stage name Eve Eden. It was the club owner who suggested it, as he felt I needed a snappier surname. I never really liked it.

Apparently there was a stripper called Eve Eden and I used to get very racy letters clearly not meant for me. Put it this way, it was a name I was very glad to get rid of.

I chose Graham as a surname as that was my grandmother's name and I wanted something memorable but at the same time to keep a name that was in the family. One grandmother was Anderson whilst the other was Graham.

I don't know why I chose the name Graham, I guess it was just random.

December 1964 – The popular top 40 music TV show *Kommotion* is first broadcast in Melbourne, Australia

It is hosted by the popular radio DJ Ken Sparkes from the Melbourne radio station 3UZ.

In August 1964 Channel 0 premiered its first pop TV programme, The Go!! Show. *The show proved such a ratings success that its original 13-episode contract was extended to 39 episodes after only seven weeks on air. As such positive momentum was achieved Channel 0 were encouraged to develop a different show that would appeal to younger viewers, hence the idea for developing* Kommotion. *Originally seen only in Melbourne, it was later syndicated to interstate stations in the newly formed 0-10 Network.*

Both Channel 0 programmes provided an alternative to the mainstream family-oriented variety format of the rival Nine Network program, Bandstand. The Go!! Show *alone regularly attracted over 400,000 teenage viewers every week.*

The Melbourne pop acts that appeared on the show included Australian hit makers Bobby & Laurie, Normie Rowe, Mike Furber, The Easybeats and The Masters Apprentices.

With purpose-made film clips only just beginning to promote records and in the absence of regular visits by major overseas acts, Kommotion, *like* Top Of The Pops, *used a troupe of young performers who danced and/or mimed to the latest hits. The producers hired a group of Melbourne teenagers, chosen for their looks, fashion sense and dancing ability. The regular cast roster included Ian 'Molly' Meldrum, who later presented* Countdown, *a programme in the 70s/80s that became the Australian equivalent of* Top Of The Pops.

For the mime segments, the producers matched the performers with a particular style of music, for instance Ian Meldrum specialised in the then-popular, high-camp 1930s style numbers such as Peter and Gordon's 'Lady Godiva' and the New Vaudeville Band's 'Winchester Cathedral'. This led to fans believing that Meldrum sang 'Winchester Cathedral'.

It was the practice of miming to hits that brought the demise of Kommotion, *as it was cancelled in early 1967 after actors' union Equity banned miming in music TV shows.*

Kommotion *was co-produced by David Joseph, who would of course soon go on to co-manage The New Seekers with Keith Potger.*

11ᵗʰ April 1965 – The Seekers perform at the *NME* Poll Winners Concert which takes place at The Empire Pool in Wembley, London

Hosted by singer Tony Bennett, The Moody Blues, Freddie and the Dreamers, Georgie Fame and the Blue Flames, Herman's Hermits, The Ivy League, Sounds Incorporated, Wayne Fontana and the Mindbenders, The Rolling Stones, Cilla Black, Donovan, Them, The Searchers, Dusty Springfield, The Animals and The Kinks are also on the bill.

Whilst by this stage The Beatles are enormous in both the US and UK, as demonstrated by the fact they win three NME awards, The Seekers are nonetheless awarded the Best New Group, with The Rolling Stones' 60s classic '(I Can't Get No) Satisfaction' the Best New Song.

15th December 1965 - The musical comedy *Charlie Girl* premieres at The Adelphi Theatre

SALLY GRAHAM (a member of the first line up of The New Seekers from 1969 to 1970): I was born in 1947 in Aldershot and lived there for a while as my father was in the army. My first steps took place in Germany, although we didn't move around a lot. At the age of six I boarded at a stage school, which I loved. By the time I was 12 my father was no longer on the scene and my mother had moved to Farnham, which I suppose you could say became my home town.

I appeared in *Charlie Girl* as a dancer for two and a half years alongside Anna Neagle, who held the lead female part of Lady Hadwell, although I was also understudy for one of Lady Hadwell's daughters. Luckily for me the girl who had the part of the daughter liked to party a lot so consequently I actually performed in that role quite a few times. I didn't really feel I was a singer and saw myself more as a dancer. However, as well as the acting and dancing I also sang as part of the crowd within that production.

16th February 1966 – The single 'You Were On My Mind' by Crispian St Peters hits a peak position of number 2 in the UK charts

This artist goes on to have another hit single in the UK with 'The Pied Piper'. Having released his first single in Australia already that year, where it reached the top 50, Marty Kristian meets Crispian on his mini tour of Melbourne. Crispian writes and produces Marty's second single 'I'll Give You Love', which is recorded at Armstrong studios, arguably the top independent recording studio of the day. Whilst not quite as successful as the first, it also reaches the Australian top 50.

MARTY KRISTIAN: I was lucky enough to be contracted with hitmaker of the time Crispian St Peters, who had a lovely country feel to his voice.

Crispian's manager was Ken Pitt. Ken was an impresario who later managed Manfred Mann and David Bowie.

Whilst recording with Crispian I struck up a friendship with Ken, who told me I should look him up if I ever came to England as he would try to help me.

28th February 1966 – *Peter Doyle's First Album* is released, distributed by Festival Records for the Queensland, Australia independent record label Sunshine Records

Still over four years away from joining that second line up of The New Seekers, it is hard to believe Peter was only 16 when his first album was released. Full of life, that Peter Doyle vocal shines through even at this early age.

MICK FLINN (who became another Australian-born member of The New Seekers from 1981 to the present): In comparison to London, Melbourne is a small place, but in the 60s it was a really rocking town.

There's always been this Sydney versus Melbourne rivalry. Sydney had nightlife but Melbourne had an underground scene. For instance there was this alternative rock music venue called The Thumpin' Tum, located at 50 Little Latrobe Street in the Melbourne CBD, managed by David Flint, which was famous locally for their toasted cheese sandwiches! There were lots of basement nightclubs, dives you could go to at midnight or sometimes even later.

Once a band had finished playing at one place they'd go somewhere else where they'd meet other musicians so they'd be able to jam all night together. On many occasions during that period, as bassist with cover band The Wild Colonials, I backed artists that included Marty Kristian and Peter Doyle. They would record a TV show and we might hang out to have a chat with them in a coffee shop or something.

I wasn't friends with either of them at that stage but we were all part of that Melbourne music scene.

We really became friends in the UK, although we certainly knew one another in Australia before that happened.

30th July 1966 – On home territory playing at Wembley Stadium, England win the football World Cup, beating Germany 4 -2 (after extra time)

They fail to reach another final until the European Championship of 2020 is held in 2021 (due to the Covid pandemic).

28th December – 'Morningtown Ride' by The Seekers reaches a peak position of number 2 in the UK charts

A song I fondly remember my eldest sister singing to me when I was very young.

29

NIC CULVERWELL (manager of The New Seekers from 2003 to the present): I was not a fan of The Seekers to the level I was a fan of The New Seekers; however, this was the first single I ever owned.

As I became older my appreciation of The Seekers grew and it was a joy to see them appear live on two occasions on their UK tour in 2014.

21st January 1967 - The first broadcast of *The Rolf Harris Show* on BBC1

At that stage Rolf was a popular Australian-born entertainer based in the UK, most famous for drawing sketches at speed, providing narrations to the audience at the same time, as well as singing Australian themed novelty records 'Tie Me Kangaroo Down Sport' and 'Sun Arise' , both of which had become top 10 hits in the UK charts earlier on in the decade.

SALLY GRAHAM: After *Charlie Girl*, I joined The Young Generation dance group. We regularly appeared on *The Rolf Harris Show* where, as fifteen boys and fifteen girls, we sang and danced.

16th February 1967 – On her 18th birthday Lynda Belcher AKA Lyn Paul is finally allowed to perform on stage in The Nocturnes; by that stage Eve Eden AKA Eve Graham had been in the group for quite a while

Signed to Columbia, The Nocturnes record singles and a studio album at Abbey Road Studios, in addition to releasing a live recording of one of their shows.

EVE GRAHAM: When Lyn auditioned, just before her 18th birthday, I was sitting out there in the dark and I was given the responsibility of choosing who should join, as Ross Mitchell, the drummer who owned the group, couldn't hear what was going on.

Lyn replaced Sandra Stevens, who later joined The Brotherhood of Man; however, Sandra stayed on as a singer in the group until Lyn became 18.

I established a friendship with Lyn straightaway. It felt like we were sisters.

23rd February 1967 - The 'I Do, I Do' 45 is The Nocturnes' first release on Columbia

The group released five more singles.

14th April 1967 – 'New York Mining Disaster 1941' is the first single release by The Bee Gees that charts in the US and UK

It is produced by Robert Stigwood and Ossie Byrne.

PAUL LAYTON: My drama school buddies called me up, telling me that we had the opportunity to audition for a group that Bees Gees producer Ossie Byrne was behind.

At the audition Ossie discovered that I was the only one that had any musical talent. For a while he became my manager and producer.

Ossie was the UK representative for Elektra records, who at that time were a private company owned by Jac Holzman. I was signed to Elektra through Ozzie. After that I went out to Los Angeles and recorded some tracks. I was introduced to the group Love for instance. When Elektra launched me in London, during that time The Doors were touring so as a promotion they decided that Jim Morrison should interview me at this house in The Mall.

Whilst The Doors were touring I was taken to their gigs. I remember the great experience of being in the wings when they played the Roundhouse in Chalk Farm.

Eventually, in 1968, the Ossie Byrne-produced Paul Layton single 'Mister, Mister'/'Sing, Sadman, Sing', with both songs written by him, was released on Paradox, a label set up specifically for the release.

30th September 1967 – BBC Radio 1 is launched in the UK to meet the demand from teenagers to hear the pop music played by pirate radio stations, when at that time the average age of the UK population was 27

Disc Jockey Tony Blackburn introduces the UK to the station as the first whole record played is 'Flowers In The Rain' by The Move. During the 70s it became the most listened-to station in the world, with listening audiences of over 10 million for some shows.

19th December 1967 – 'Emerald City' by Australian group The Seekers reaches a UK chart peak position of 50

This is the group's last UK hit in the sixties, having achieved two number ones, four top tens and two top twenties in the charts there between 1965 to 1967.

14th February 1968 – During a tour of New Zealand, Judith Durham tells the other group members she is leaving The Seekers to pursue a solo career

KEITH POTGER: To me this wasn't a shock at all as Judith was a solo singer before she joined The Seekers.

I had actually expected that she would one day return to a solo career.

MARTY KRISTIAN: On the set of *The Go!! Show* friend and fellow singer Colin Cook told me he was soon off to England with the journey paid for as he was to sing in a duo on a ship called the *Fairstar*. I told him straight away that I wished I could join him. Soon after this I ran into him again in Collins Street, Melbourne. He told me that his partner could no longer go as he had been called up for National Service in Vietnam. Asking me if I'd be still interested in coming to England - I bit his hand off, joining him in a singing duo on the ship.

Arriving in the UK in 1968, I contacted Ken Pitt, who told me I could stay at a flat he owned as the current resident was moving out the day before our arrival. Ken Pitt picked myself and Colin up as soon as we got off the ship, taking us over to the flat in London. I discovered the person moving out of the flat was David Bowie.

David came to the flat several times. One time I even played guitar with him in the kitchen. My memory of David was that he was a nice guy but he had something of a chip on his shoulder about Marc Bolan, a character more successful than he was at that time.

I think David felt he was more deserving of the success Marc was currently enjoying.

KEITH POTGER: I had started writing songs so I was also interested in pursuing some sort of solo career myself. As with Judith, I had also been doing some solo stuff before The Seekers, so it had always been in the back of mind to continue with that too. However, at that point in time, unlike the other members of The Seekers, I was very much a family man and by then we'd just had our son Matthew.

Having a young family was an important factor for me to consider with anything I chose to do.

July 1968 - Judith Durham leaves The Seekers to pursue a solo career and the group officially disband

KEITH POTGER: After the group disbanded, Athol and Bruce returned to Australia. Judith, having met the man she would later marry, was from memory then based in Switzerland, whilst I was the only member of the group that resided in the UK.

Having renewed contact with David Joseph, who was by now over here in the UK promoting Normie Rowe and The Playboys, in June of '68 after a few glasses of red wine we discussed what I should do when The Seekers broke up. Consequently David and I set up Leon Henry Productions together, which eventually became the London based Toby Organisation. Initially it was a very casual thing and it wasn't really even a business arrangement. We were just looking at what might happen if I was to do some solo work.

To begin with we came up with the idea of Normie Rowe's backing band The Playboys becoming the backing band for me. Rehearsals at the back end of 1968 leading into the early part of 1969 went quite well; however, the group decided they wanted to go it alone, changing their name to Procession.

For a short while Ross Wilson is lead vocalist of that group, an individual who is most famed in Australia for producing Skyhooks and writing 'Eagle Rock' whilst a member of Daddy Cool, a song often referred to as The Australian Alternative National Anthem.

As well as this the (so far) last top 30 UK hit for The New Seekers in 1985 is an interpretation of a Procession song.

Whilst the partnership with The Playboys ended amicably, somehow the idea came to us both that instead of finding a backing group we should look to establish a whole new group. That was where the idea came to create The New Seekers.

Whilst The New Seekers are yet to be born, the concept of the group is born... and their story begins...

34

Chapter 2
1969: The New Seekers Mark One - Chris, Eve, Laurie, Marty and Sally

IN THE UK IN 1969...
The Spacehopper, a bouncy orange toy, looking like an oversized balloon rabbit, is first introduced * Australian media mogul Rupert Murdoch purchases the popular Sunday newspaper *News Of The World* * Matt Busby retires as manager of Manchester United * Pop star Lulu marries Bee Gee Maurice Gibb * Beatle John marries Yoko, Beatle Paul marries Linda * Popular children's bike, the robust Raleigh Chopper, is introduced * Brian Jones, founder member of The Rolling Stones, dies * The Battle of The Bogside breaks out, the first major confrontation in The Troubles of Northern Ireland * The abolition of the death penalty in the UK is made permanent

30th January – The Beatles perform on the roof of their Apple Corps Headquarters at 3 Savile Row in London
Lasting forty-two minutes, it is their last ever live performance.

March 1969 – With The Seekers disbanding, The New Seekers project is shaped by Keith Potger and David Joseph

KEITH POTGER: My focus was the music side whilst David's focus was more the business side.

MARTY KRISTIAN: Colin Cook came up to me one day telling me I had to see this lady fortune teller who he thought was amazing. I was quite sceptical but nevertheless he had fired up my imagination so I decided to find out what it was all about by going to see this Mrs Knowles character.

Going over to where she lived in Marylebone Street was an incredible experience. She told me exact details about this school friend who nearly died as well as describing the items on my mantelpiece, even correctly telling me the number of my house.

Mrs Knowles also told me that around the time of my birthday major changes were going to happen in my life. The number 5 would be very important. Apparently I was going to be offered a situation where I was

35

going to travel all the time but at the end of the first year of this project I would want to throw everything away. She advised me that if I could stick it out it would be the best thing for me. Mrs Knowles saw me standing in front of a sea of people and told me that I was going to be more successful than I could have ever imagined. A very short, dark haired man, full of energy and enthusiasm, would be important in my life. She saw a capital D. I wondered what she was talking about.

Soon afterwards I got a call from David Joseph, a short, dark haired man who wanted me to join this group called The New Seekers with four other people.

I'd already developed a relationship with David Joseph, running across him through *The Go!! Show* in Melbourne, and I knew Keith Potger. Somehow David found out I was in England and tracked me down. With The Seekers disbanding they told me that they wanted to establish another group in a similar style calling it The New Seekers. Instead of having one girl, producing that distinctive sound that The Seekers had with Judith, they wanted two girls, and David wanted me to join the group.

KEITH POTGER: We both knew Marty Kristian. I didn't know him as well as David did, as he had been a producer on those TV shows Marty had performed on.

MARTY KRISTIAN: With Colin Cook I was rehearsing a production of *Hair* when the opportunity to join The New Seekers came along. I had to make a decision between the two options and eventually chose the group as David Joseph was very, very persuasive.

SALLY GRAHAM: I had been doing a lot of commercials and TV shows. In fact when Keith Potger rang me about the audition I was working for the BBC as a dancer on *The David Jacobs Show*, which as a format was two girls and three boys dancing to the hit record of the week whilst he interviewed people. Again singing wasn't really 'my thing' at that point as I was more of a dancer (originally I wanted to be a ballerina).

At the time Marty Kristian was considering The New Seekers, from my understanding he was also going to audition for an understudy part in a musical. Marty Kristian had told David Toguri, the choreographer who had been coaching him (the choreographer who worked with me in *Charlie Girl* who would eventually be the choreographer on *The Rocky Horror Show*), about this 'New Seekers Project', explaining they were looking for two girls and three boys who could sing as well as 'dance a bit'. David thought of me and passed my phone details on to Marty, who in turn passed them on to Keith.

36

When Keith called me I thought it was someone having a joke!

EVE GRAHAM: Ultimately I was keen on joining The New Seekers as it was a five part vocal group and I loved singing harmony. However I was just as happy in The Nocturnes as I was in The New Seekers to start with.

Nobody knew at that stage how big the group was going to be.

CHRIS BARRINGTON: I had been accepted at The Royal Academy of Dramatic Art (RADA) and I was already doing very well as a jobbing actor, with people on the bus even asking me for my autograph, when this offer came along. It was my best mate Laurie Heath that instigated it.

Writing songs, he always wanted to go in a musical direction. Laurie Heath had already successfully auditioned and without me knowing anything about it he put my name forward too for the bass player position. I had no real interest in joining a band although being in one held a lot of currency at that time with what was happening with The Beatles.

In those days it seemed as though everybody played guitar. However, although I played acoustic guitar I had never picked up a bass in my life.

KEITH POTGER: In setting up The New Seekers with David Joseph we decided there had to be female involvement. We wanted this new group to be different and distinct from the original Seekers purely and simply because there would be two females. In those days it was unusual to have two female singers in a group even though in the US there had been The Mamas & Papas. Arguably Abba followed that New Seekers format.

EVE GRAHAM: I had left The Nocturnes by the time I auditioned for The New Seekers and I was in Manchester singing with another group.

KEITH POTGER: For the female singers we put adverts in *Melody Maker* and the *New Musical Express (NME)*. Sally Graham and Eve Graham both responded to those ads. I clearly remember Eve coming over to my place and introducing herself, stating she had come in response to the advertisement. It was great as it was such a basic process in those days.

At the audition as I recall I didn't ask Eve to sing The Seekers' song 'Georgy Girl' or anything like that [laughing]!

Once Eve started singing I was blown away by her voice.

KEITH POTGER: Quite quickly we had a lynch pin in Marty and then very soon after we had another lynch pin in Eve.

Having those two lynch pins made it a little easier to decide on who else should make the final cut.

CHRIS BARRINGTON: I auditioned for the bass player role, having never picked up a bass in my life, by just showing up at Keith's apartment. I remember going into the room and playing two or three verses of The Everly Brothers song 'Devoted To You' on an acoustic. With that it would have been clear to Keith I could sing and play a few chords.

I was really surprised when I got the call that I was in the group but it was fun as I was just 19!

KEITH POTGER: As with Paul Layton who replaced him, Chris Barrington in the first line up learnt to play the bass pretty much from scratch. They both did tremendously well as that electric bass was a key component in the sound for the group.

We decided from the outset we didn't want an acoustic bass player.

CHRIS BARRINGTON: I had to learn the bass quickly. They wanted us to be able to sing but they weren't too concerned about our musical ability.

KEITH POTGER: We wanted this new line up to not just be singers like The Seekers had been but for group members to have capabilities in other directions, including, for example, a capacity to dance.

Chris Barrington, Laurie Heath and Sally Graham were all chosen as they had dancing as a string to their bow. They were wonderful movers as far as choreography was concerned but also very good singers and good instrumentalists as well. Sally had a lovely, true voice for instance yet she didn't have the power that Eve had.

CHRIS BARRINGTON: Sally had a professional dance background. The school I attended with Laurie was a drama and dance school. We were tap dancers and did all kinds of stuff. We knew how to move on stage for sure.

I knew some chords but I wasn't a great guitar player.

SALLY GRAHAM: When I told my friends I'd been offered an audition for The New Seekers, after I explained what it was, they told me not to go along as to them it sounded really corny.

At that time, apart from working at the BBC, I was perceived by my friends as being very cool in having a stall on Kensington Market, a flat in Notting Hill Gate and driving a Mustang! Whilst I didn't realise it then, looking back now I had arrived! Did I really want to sing 'Morningtown Ride' in a pop group wearing horrible dresses (which is what lay ahead of me)? I went to the audition out of curiosity partly as I really wanted to see if the guy behind it really was the one from The Seekers!

KEITH POTGER: We were looking more for an attitude and whether each person auditioning thought this would be an opportunity for them.

SALLY GRAHAM: When I went round and Keith opened the door I said 'you're the handsome one in the Seekers with the guitar [laughing]!'
Basically the two of us sat down singing Everly Brothers harmonies, which I remembered from those days with my sister, as these were the only harmonising songs we both knew.
I auditioned at his beautiful house in Hamilton Terrace, Maida Vale, near St John's Terrace.

KEITH POTGER: Let's face it, the original Seekers were a middle of the road, homey sort of act and were certainly not rock 'n' roll or hip, like The Animals, The Stones or The Beatles. To actually want to be in a circumstance that was pretty middle of the road required a certain type of attitude, so that's what David and I were looking for more than anything else. We weren't really looking for a folk sensibility as we wanted to move the group on into more of a pop realm with acoustic instruments, more along the lines of what Cat Stevens was doing at that time I suppose.

SALLY GRAHAM: My memory is that we were told it would be the same format as The Seekers but this time round there would be sketches and a bit of dancing too.

CHRIS BARRINGTON: I felt it was important to Keith with the project that everybody looked good on stage.
We went to a professional hairdresser called Leonards and we had all our stage suits tailor made. It was very much about 'projecting an image'. Sally, Laurie and myself had stage presence, as had Marty and Eve. Before The New Seekers Marty had a music career in Australia and Eve had been singing for a while in the UK.
It was that 'professional look' that they wanted, which all five of us had.

KEITH POTGER: I would say in all we auditioned less than a dozen people for that first line up of The New Seekers [note - whilst Lyn Paul unsuccessfully auditioned for that first line up, in conversation with me Keith did not remember that].

EVE GRAHAM: When I was in that first line up of The New Seekers I didn't have any contact with Lyn but then we ended up living in the same house down in London, although she was sharing with another girl.

In the earliest days of The New Seekers at that time she was trying to establish a solo career.

PAUL LAYTON: Laurie Heath and Chris Barrington were old drama school buddies of mine at The Ada Foster Theatre School. For instance, when I started at the school I remember Laurie appearing in the stage production of *Oliver*.

Had I not been trying to launch my solo career in the US on Elektra at that time I believe the project might have been something I would have been put forward to do.

CHRIS BARRINGTON: On joining The New Seekers I was paid six pounds a week. I had to sign nine different contracts. I signed those contracts without reading them because I guess I was 19.

SALLY GRAHAM: I only have a vague memory of the finance we received, however we were all given a piece of paper as a contract, which they advised us to check, and I know I probably should have done that.

I guess I was a bit flippant about the project as I was still working at the BBC and contracted there too, so with that I had the attitude I didn't need to be a New Seeker.

I was very lucky as I had an uncle who was a partner in a solicitor's firm that had died in a plane crash and along with my sister we were his sole beneficiaries. With that situation I was already financially self-sufficient.

MICK FLINN: When we signed with David and Keith in the early part of the next decade we were paid more than Chris Barrington remembers receiving but from that salary we each had to fund our accommodation and living costs. What we were paid didn't go far.

The management paid for what we needed for our stage performances (for instance our hair and clothing). As we were topping the bill where we played, we always stayed in the best hotels.

We were treated like stars in that sense even though we weren't.

KEITH POTGER: We intended to bring the musicality of The Seekers into the 70s (and hopefully even into the 80s) but at the same time go into the American market more solidly than had been the case with the original group.

To start with, the group very much had a British angle, but then as the group progressed offices were opened in Los Angeles. The whole project eventually followed a very interesting trajectory.

CHRIS BARRINGTON: When we joined The New Seekers, Sally, Laurie and myself thought we would be allowed to make an input creatively but we weren't. Nevertheless as a young 19-year-old I had fun!

SALLY GRAHAM: I always regarded Laurie Heath as being incredibly talented as a songwriter.

June – After rehearsals at St Mark's Church Hall, Hamilton Terrace, in the London suburb of St John's Wood, David Joseph and Keith Potger decide The New Seekers are ready to be unveiled to the public

CHRIS BARRINGTON: All five of us could sing really well.

KEITH POTGER: I rehearsed that first line up very rigorously.

SALLY GRAHAM: Initially I regularly arrived at rehearsals really late as I was still working as a dancer at the BBC.

CHRIS BARRINGTON: We rehearsed every day at a place in London near Keith's house. We'd sit down and go through the music. Keith would instruct us on what we were going to do. After that we'd sit around and play the songs.

SALLY GRAHAM: I remember rehearsing an Al Jolson medley and just thinking 'why not?' To me it was something to do that was different so I went along with it.

CHRIS BARRINGTON: The atmosphere was pretty good. We all got along with each other well. Keith taught me the basics of the bass guitar.

SALLY GRAHAM: It was quite school-like in the sense we had to sit in these little chairs.

Keith was really nice to us and it was good fun. However when David Joseph came in it was like a black cloud appeared. For instance if we were talking to each other whilst he was talking to Keith he'd tell us to be quiet. Although we were adults he used to call us 'kids'!

We didn't see David very often. I didn't get the impression we were his sole priority.

CHRIS BARRINGTON: We did enjoy it. Basically it was fun as it was nice hanging around with a bunch of people playing music. Keith was a good teacher.

SALLY GRAHAM: The rehearsals were very much a 9 to 5 commitment.

Chris Barrington was the joker in the pack, pulling very funny faces. It was difficult for me not to laugh as Chris and Laurie were always mucking around. Together they were both terribly, terribly funny. They were playing to me as their audience.

The fact that Eve and Marty didn't think they were funny made me laugh even more.

KEITH POTGER: As they started to gel consequently David and myself felt confident The New Seekers project would work well.

CHRIS BARRINGTON: Laurie was my best mate and Sally had a great sense of humour. We both always got on with Sally so well. In fact Sally, Laurie and myself soon became as thick as thieves.

SALLY GRAHAM: We were a different breed to Marty and Eve as the three of us had been to stage school. We'd worked professionally already in films, TV and theatre. In that sense all three of us felt we already knew what we were doing and I felt David Joseph didn't take account of that.

CHRIS BARRINGTON: We'd got work as professional performers on TV previous to joining The New Seekers. That drew us all together but on reflection I think we were perhaps too much of a three person clique.

SALLY GRAHAM: We were all thrown together. I got on fine with Marty and Eve. To begin with it was all of us siding against David Joseph but then it was Chris, Laurie and myself in a gang more than the other two.

Although we were adults it was like we had a strict headteacher in David Joseph whilst Keith Potger was our friendly, smiling teacher. I felt both characters were so different in personality it was hard to imagine the two of them were ever actually friends!

20th July – Although conspiracy theories may now suggest otherwise, Neil Armstrong becomes the first human being to set foot on the Earth's moon

Famously, as the whole world seems to be watching in black and white TV, apparently Neil delivers his line of 'that's one small step for a man but one giant leap for mankind' correctly as he steps onto the surface of the moon, although the feed is such no one hears the word 'a'.

15th August to 18th August – The Woodstock Open Air Concert takes place in the US

Over 500,000 people supposedly enjoy a festival of love, peace and music.

16th August – The first TV appearance of 'Keith Potger and the New Seekers'

The first five-piece New Seekers line up consists of three males, Laurie Heath, Chris Barrington and Marty Kristian, with two females, Eve Graham and Sally Graham. With their first TV performance alongside drag artist Danny La Rue, they appear on The Frankie Howerd Show, *on ITV in the UK.*

Frankie Howerd performs stand up comedy in the show and reaches the peak of his fame in the early seventies as the central character Lurcio in the historical comedy Up Pompeii. *However he is probably best remembered for appearing in several Carry On films, each one housing typically British suggestive humour seemingly popular at that time.*

SALLY GRAHAM: For that show I remember that going into make-up they drew black eyebrows on me. I was upset by that as I couldn't remove them after the performance!

CHRIS BARRINGTON: The girls had to wear frilly dresses that went from the neck to the floor whilst the boys had to always wear the same formal suits. We had to have our hair a certain way before we performed on stage. The image had to be just right.

43

SALLY GRAHAM: Strangely the early bespoke beige and maroon suits that the boys wore on stage were tailor made for them through my stall at Kensington Market.

With us all living in London, one time the management flew us to Edinburgh in order that myself and Eve could choose fabric from a department store there for tailor made dresses. Maroon velvet was chosen for the upper round neck, high waisted section of the dress, with stripy gold curtain-like material for the skirt. Not very stylish in my opinion. I would have thought it would have been more sensible if they asked us to buy a couple of Ossie Clark dresses in London.

Although The New Seekers wore more casual clothes later on after I left I've often wondered why, to start with, they wanted the boys to wear suits and us to be wearing these extraordinary Victorian governess type dresses? What you look like on stage really determines the kind of audience you're going to get, I think, which meant to begin with we weren't appealing to the younger generation.

I think they wanted us to portray a wholesome image, appealing to the mums and dads. Keith was focusing on attracting an audience from those people that held fond memories of The Seekers and keeping the continuity going with them.

KEITH POTGER: I must say we had two very fine booking agents in Slim and Freya Miller [who eventually went on to manage Shakin' Stevens to excellent effect] that were very much part of Team New Seekers and they gave us huge assistance securing those spots on the popular TV shows of the time.

Slim had been a stand up comedian and had a good reputation so when he went into agency work he took with him a whole bunch of connections, which was good for the acts he worked with. On the other hand, The New Seekers were a bloody good group who could deliver the goods.

CHRIS BARRINGTON: Keith really wanted The New Seekers project to work.

17ᵗʰ August - The first live show of Keith Potger and the New Seekers
This takes place at The Pavilion in Bournemouth, UK.

SALLY GRAHAM: For our debut we stayed at a hotel owned by the parents-in-law of Keith Potger!

Before our first formal concert I remember we had played an unadvertised practice gig at a pub in the New Forest.

KEITH POTGER: In my view I wasn't ever in the group, but I guess it's in the eye of the beholder really.

In terms of live performances I would do one or two songs at the front then nick off [note - Australian term] and leave the group to do the show, coming back on in joining them for the finale. I would play banjo for instance, something that the group couldn't yet do. That was it really as the whole idea was that The New Seekers were those five people in a group whereas I was just 'Keith Potger'.

SALLY GRAHAM: My belief is Keith performed to start with as that gave the project credibility as he had been one of The Seekers.

It would have been wrong calling the group The New Seekers without there at least being one of The Seekers within it.

KEITH POTGER: The plan for The New Seekers was that I would perform alongside the group but that I would only do that for a short period at the start, maybe six months or something like that. Like an introductory offer to the public at large if you will!

SALLY GRAHAM: Knowing Keith as I do, The New Seekers project wasn't anything to do with his ego, as he was a really nice bloke!

It was a huge help for us getting started that the group was known as 'Keith Potger and the New Seekers', otherwise I'm sure we would have struggled with bookings.

MARTY KRISTIAN: In terms of performing, Keith was on the periphery. He'd have his spot when he'd play then let us do our own thing, eventually receding into a management role.

CHRIS BARRINGTON: The places we played at to begin with were not always well suited to our act.

SALLY GRAHAM: I felt the material we were given to perform wasn't very good at all.

CHRIS BARRINGTON: For instance we'd be playing a very middle of the road feel good song like 'Happy Heart' by Andy Williams, a US number 1 that year celebrating the concept of being on holiday, at rugged working men's clubs in the North of England.

45

SALLY GRAHAM: In those Northern working men's clubs they paid absolutely no attention to us when we were introduced to the audience at the start of our act. They'd all be drinking, smoking and talking, which would continue throughout the performance.

If they liked us they threw beer mats towards us on the stage which I guess took the place of applause.

CHRIS BARRINGTON: The material was totally wrong for those types of venues.

SALLY GRAHAM: We often had to change in a room full of beer bottles.

I remember once this man, who was doing a performance on the same bill as us where he was 'tap dancing on roller skates', being chased by a debt collector; he ran into our room and jumped out the window to get away from him. The atmosphere was always pretty weird at these places.

CHRIS BARRINGTON: We also played at GI bases in Germany, with soldiers there about to go off to Vietnam, and I remember we were booed off stage. Bottles were even thrown at us.

SALLY GRAHAM: They had all been enjoying listening to James Brown before we came on whilst we were performing songs like 'Georgy Girl'. They didn't want to hear us.

CHRIS BARRINGTON: I felt we were sometimes playing material like 'Happy Heart' that none of us wanted to do.

SALLY GRAHAM: I was never nervous about performing, instead I was more concerned whether the audience liked what we were doing and how we compared to The Seekers. Would we be accepted?

KEITH POTGER: I pretty much financed The New Seekers to start with.

They were each paid a stipend to keep the wolf from the door based on both sides delivering (us as the management and the individuals in the group) what was agreed.

Each member of The New Seekers had a contract. I discussed the financial side of things with David Joseph but he oversaw the management of all that.

Situated in West Yorkshire, the club became a major venue on the North of England variety club circuit.

During its existence concerts by performers including Louis Armstrong, Shirley Bassey, Tom Jones, Roy Orbison, Eartha Kitt, Gene Pitney, Neil Sedaka and Ken Dodd were staged there. At the peak of its success, the club had 300,000 members. It closed in 1978, reopening as Crumpets night club.

James and Betty Corrigan had travelled to Las Vegas to research how the clubs worked there in order to come up with a design for Batley. The club was built in early 1967 on top of a disused sewage site on Bradford Road. Construction took three months from start to finish, with floodlights erected so construction workers could work through the night to meet the deadline for opening on Easter Sunday. The build was interrupted when local authority inspectors discovered that the structure was six inches too close to the road. Demolition took place and work continued but, despite this setback, the club managed to open on 27 March 1967 as planned.

The headline act on opening night was vocal harmony group The Bachelors.

KEITH POTGER: With David we had the ambitious idea of setting up a film set so we could record the whole performance at Batley and of course with the line up change this effectively very quickly became archival footage.

The real tragedy is that footage has now been lost! It was filmed carefully in 35mm, with special set ups for sound and lighting. Where that footage has gone nobody knows!

NIC CULVERWELL: The Batley film of The New Seekers wasn't particularly well promoted though of course The Batley Variety Club was an important venue on the circuit in those days. I remember going to see the New Seekers film as a support movie with *The Exorcist*.

SALLY GRAHAM: I remember seeing it in Notting Hill Gate as a B movie paired with another film but that film was most certainly NOT *The Exorcist*!

NIC CULVERWELL: I know the film is now held at The British Film Institute for purchase by the manager of the group or the artists themselves. Keith is wrong in believing it's been lost - however, it is an expensive purchase!

DONNA JONES: Winning Granada TV's competition 'First Timers' for 'the best new female singer' helped me gain a solo recording contract at MCA when I was still a teenager. I recorded songs in London with Mike Leander producing and released the single 'Heaven Held'. I didn't sing any of my own material, the songs were all covers. My big song was Edith Piaf's 'No Regrets'.

Before my time in The New Seekers I had been Manchester focused with my singing career, until I got a new manager who was determined that I should break into the cabaret scene. However, unfortunately I couldn't drive. I'd sometimes travel at night, playing at three clubs, going from one to the other; in those days I could afford a taxi. My manager gave me an ultimatum by stating I have booked you to play at the prestigious Batley Variety Club in three months' time so you'll need to learn to drive. As a consequence I took a crash course and passed my test so I could get over to Batley.

That was a real kick up the pants for me but on the other hand I was very independent.

October – 'Meet My Lord' becomes the first ever release by The New Seekers

With songwriting for the A side credited to J.Kelly, the Laurie Heath song 'Zarzis' is on the flip side, with lyrics about his memories of this

48

coastal commune in Tunisia. The publishing for the B side is held with the
Leon Henry/Carlin Music Corporation.
  The single, produced by Keith Potger, does not chart.

NIC CULVERWELL: The title of the first single release 'Meet My Lord' perhaps inappropriately points a potential record buyer towards the group being religiously oriented; however, the song itself is strong.

SALLY GRAHAM: I remember listening to the scratchy noise of our first single on Keith's transistor radio on the pavement in a Blackburn street during the period we were playing those northern clubs.

NIC CULVERWELL: Eve sounds great on it and the song accentuates her as the lead vocalist of the group. If that song had become a hit they may well have continued in that folk direction.

SALLY GRAHAM: I accepted from the outset Eve would be the lead singer. I'm a vocal harmoniser and always have been!

CHRIS BARRINGTON: We did what we were told. The group were given the material they had to perform and the group performed it.

MICK FLINN: In the days of Springfield Revival, when we were managed by Keith Potger and David Joseph in the early 70s, we had to rehearse like hell, constantly repeating harmony parts for instance. From my understanding of that first line up with the three that left they were Londoners who thought they were 'too cool for school' to keep going like that.
  I feel with the experience Eve and Marty had already, they knew where this project could take them and in that sense they had faith in the management team, which of course paid dividends in the end as after the three that left the first line up The New Seekers became hugely successful.

5th October – The first ever episode of *Monty Python* is broadcast on BBC1
  It had been recorded on the 7th September and in total 45 episodes of the series were broadcast. Monty Python projects a zany surrealistic sense of humour regarded as typically British. However, the animations, also an integral part of the brand, came from an American, Terry Gilliam, who goes onto direct hugely expensive films.

49

15th November – The first programme in colour is broadcast by the BBC in the UK

This was Petula Clark's concert at the Royal Albert Hall in London.

6th December – The Rolling Stones play Altamont Freeway

Notorious for the death of Meredith Hunter at the hands of the Hell's Angels, this is the moment, some would say, when the peace and love vibe of the sixties ends.

Staying at the top of the charts for eight weeks the bubblegum pop of 'Sugar, Sugar' by manufactured group The Archies was 1969's best selling song in the UK.

Chapter 3
January to June 1970: The Aquarian Age? The Road Towards Perfect Line Up Harmony

IN THE UK IN 1970…

A 747 is the first ever jumbo jet to land in Britain * Black Sabbath release their debut album, launching the Heavy Metal genre * The duo Tyrannosaurus Rex including Marc Bolan headline The Worthy Pop Festival in Glastonbury with an estimated 1500 people attending * Harold Wilson's Labour Party is defeated in the UK General Election as the Conservatives led by Ted Heath come to power * Riots break out in Londonderry, Northern Ireland over the arrest of Mid-Ulster MP Bernadette Devlin * The guitarist Jimi Hendrix dies * The first British page three girl appears in The Sun newspaper

January – The New Seekers release their first album, simply entitled *The New Seekers*

With Laurie Heath and Marty Kristian each contributing two songs, the other nine songs are interpretations. This album is produced by Keith Potger as he shares the arrangements with John Barham and Graham Hall.

Eve Graham contributes lead vocals on four tracks whilst Laurie, Marty, Sally and Chris take lead vocals on two tracks each.

A FAN'S PERSPECTIVE ON THE ALBUM: As shown by the cover photograph of the group, with the male members wearing formal matching beige suits whilst the females wear neck to floor dresses, it was an album directed towards The Seekers' audience. With that photograph messaging The New Seekers as a group most comfortable playing live, rather incongruously they quickly became a group associated with TV performances. At that point in time the group had yet to find a defined style or clear direction that suited them.

The album has two of Eve Graham's finest vocals in 'Angel Of The Morning' and 'Something's Gotten A Hold Of My Heart'. Whilst Sally Graham gets a look in she isn't projected as a lead vocalist. As the male members of the group aren't brought to the fore vocally the album is very much a vehicle for Eve.

51

EVE GRAHAM: As time went on we were brought some great songs from some great people. I was never a songwriter and never got involved in any of that. I'm inclined to believe Marty's songs were included on that album to entice him to stay in the group.

MARTY KRISTIAN: In those days I received no encouragement to write songs for the group, as basically the material was provided for us. Every now and then we'd put songs up for consideration. If they were chosen that was great but it was like a bonus.

CHRIS BARRINGTON: Keith really wanted to make an input to the music which is how he got to produce the first album. I felt there were some strange song selections on that album.

MICK FLINN: To me, with that first album Keith seemed to be trying to fill a gap that The Seekers had left by going in that folk direction but also with that cabaret style which would have gone down well on the live circuit.

NIC CULVERWELL: I absolutely love that first album. For me it was the ideal release if you were looking to target The Seekers' audience along with an inquisitive new fan base.

As it was released before the days of The New Seekers appearing regularly on TV that partly explains why it wasn't a commercial success.

KEITH POTGER: From an early stage with those recordings Eve always hit the mark with her vocals as she was a tremendous singer. What a voice! Her professional attitude, from the time I first met her at my London flat to when I stopped dealing with her, never wavered. That was to be expected as Eve had previously sung in The Nocturnes.

SALLY GRAHAM: A song like 'Angel Of The Morning' would be brought in but they wouldn't be looking at me for a lead vocal on the song. They'd be focussing on Eve, who would learn the lead vocal and then we'd all do the harmonies. Linking back to The Seekers, it was largely set up as Eve being that central Judith Durham figure in taking the lead vocal.

They did let me sing lead vocals on a song from that album, Bob Dylan's 'Too Much of Nothing', where I sort of droned on a bit [laughing]! I'm alright in a crowd and with harmonies but the thing is I'm not a professionally trained singer.

KEITH POTGER: Early on we tried to create a buzz for the group so that songwriters brought us their best material. It was a case of ramping things up and luckily Phillips put money behind the group for that first recording. It became a calling card for the group and a platform to build from.

However, running alongside that was the growing sense Laurie, Chris and Sally were not feeling comfortable with the project.

SALLY GRAHAM: The three of us weren't particularly discontented with the project at this point in time and just knuckled down with the recording.

At that point we certainly weren't looking to leave The New Seekers.

CHRIS BARRINGTON: The discontent from Sally, Laurie and I with what we were being asked to do was growing gradually all the time.

SALLY GRAHAM: Laurie had been told he could contribute songs to The New Seekers but in the next breath we were asked to learn 'The Sound Of Music Medley'. However it was very entertaining and people seemed to like it.

We never thought we'd be doing that sort of material though.

KEITH POTGER: There was tension there which really didn't help the group's cause and early that year the musical tectonic plates started to shift.

SALLY GRAHAM: From my perspective, when David Joseph turned up at rehearsals he put a dampener on things.

To start with we accepted the idea of performing the material we had been given, even though we didn't really like it. However, more and more Laurie Heath started to write songs. I guess the three of us psychologically began to get in a huddle. We started to learn his material and, without telling the other two, decided that we should think about doing our own thing.

CHRIS BARRINGTON: Speaking on behalf of Sally and Laurie, The New Seekers project for us was really 'hokey'. For instance, we didn't enjoy tap dancing on stage or performing those barber shop quartet pieces.

From my memory, away from the singing, David Joseph asked me the question 'what else can you do' and because the response was 'well I can tap dance' it was just randomly thrown into the act.

SALLY GRAHAM: Chris mentioned tap dancing as a joke and never expected that comment to be taken seriously in the way David Joseph took it.

CHRIS BARRINGTON: Essentially we were told what to do, where to go and what to play.

3rd January – Jon Pertwee becomes the third Doctor Who, debuting in the first episode of the 'Spearhead From Space' series on BBC1
For the first time this groundbreaking and popular sci-fi TV series is broadcast to the nation in colour.

10th January – Blue Mink single 'Melting Pot' peaks at number 3 in the UK charts
A Cook and Greenaway song, Blue Mink was established by keyboardist Roger Coulam.

Roger Cook and black US soul singer Madeline Bell, who contributed backing vocals to The Rolling Stones classic 'You Can't Always Get What You Want', were co lead vocalists on single releases.

With the ethos of people being together 'in perfect harmony', 'Melting Pot' is very much in keeping with the brand The New Seekers stood for, albeit, by today's standards, it does contain some unfortunate slang that might quite rightly be construed as racist language.

'Melting Pot' was the group's second release and first hit single. Blue Mink continued their hit making run in the UK until 1973. Another notable song is 'Banner Man', which has the same celebratory ethos as 'Melting Pot'. It also goes on to a peak position of number 3 in the UK charts at a time just before The New Seekers reached their 1972 commercial peak.

KEITH POTGER: Roger Cook came to see me when I was rehearsing the group in the St Mark's Church Hall with the song 'Melting Pot' and we all loved it.

SALLY GRAHAM: I remember Roger Cook coming to our rehearsals as someone who Eve knew. He just banged out this incredible song on the piano that we all thought was marvellous.

From my understanding he essentially brought the song along for us to perform but David Joseph turned it down for us.

We all wanted to do the song, including Keith.

KEITH POTGER: We were spewing [note - Australian for 'very annoyed'] when we heard it on the radio after it had been released with Roger singing the lead vocals as one of Blue Mink.

8th February – The New Seekers play The Queen Elizabeth Hall at London's Southbank

PAUL LAYTON: That day my producer, Ossie Byrne, took me to see The New Seekers perform and in the interval ironically he bumped into Peter Doyle, a person he knew, who was over in the UK playing with The Virgil Brothers. That was the very first time I met Peter. It was amazing to think that in just over four months we would both be in the group we came to hear and watch that night!

I loved the professionalism of what The New Seekers were doing. It was great. At that time they were very much a variety act as, for instance, they sang barber shop and a Jolson medley, material that we took on to begin with in that mark two line up of The New Seekers.

22nd February – The single release 'United We Stand' by The Brotherhood of Man reaches a peak position of 10 in the UK chart

The Brotherhood of Man, here with their second single release after their debut 'Love One Another' failed to chart, have characteristics in common with The New Seekers, most notably a three male, two female vocal dynamic. At this point in time the group consists of Roger Greenaway, soon to be renowned for his writing partnership with Roger Cook, who is now vocalist in Blue Mink, Tony Burrows and John Goodison, who are also both songwriters, Sue Glover and Sunny Leslie (who in reality actually hold the same surname, being sisters).

As with The New Seekers, they are a manufactured group, and the brainchild behind them is UK producer/songwriter Tony Hiller. In fact Hiller co-wrote this song with group member John Goodison (who uses the pseudonym Peter Simons) with Goodison going on to co-write The Bay City Rollers' second UK number one 'Give A Little Love' with Phil Wainman.

The song itself is quite different in style to The New Seekers template as it is something of a soft rock anthem with a rousing vocal. It's a great song and should have charted higher than that number 10 position. Although the next single, 'Where Are You Going To My Love', reaches number 22 in the charts, it will be some time (and after Eurovision success) before this group has another UK hit.

14ᵗʰ March – Mary Hopkins appears on BBC1's *It's Cliff* singing 'Knock Knock Who's There' which the great British public have voted as their choice for *A Song For Europe*, a precursor of The Eurovision Song Contest

The series It's Cliff *debuted on the 3ʳᵈ January 1970. By this stage Cliff Richard is already developing into something of a legend, having experienced dozens of hits. To start with, most especially with his debut 'Move It', he is regarded as a British Elvis. However, particularly with the UK number 1 hit 'Congratulations', which is runner up in the 1968 Eurovision Song Contest, his songs now appeal to a wide range of age groups. At this point in time with his younger fans he is perhaps most highly regarded for his lead role in the often repeated light comedy 60s feel good film* Summer Holiday. *His backing band The Shadows have had numerous hits without Cliff. The bespectacled Hank Marvin, perhaps the most famous member of the group, appears on the show.*

The format of the show consists of Cliff Richard (and his guests) singing songs. As well as this he performs in sketches (sometimes with his musical guests), with actress Una Stubbs, who also appeared in Summer Holiday, *as a mainstay alongside him. With the show broadcast at a prime time spot for the British watching audience, as some people in those days even refuse to watch programmes on the rival ITV station, an appearance on the show acts as incredible promotion for artists as they are regarded as being endorsed by Cliff (and by extension the BBC itself).*

21st March – Dana wins the Eurovision Song Contest for Ireland with 'All Kinds Of Everything'

A contest that is very popular with British TV audiences, the song becomes a UK number 1, whilst the UK entrant, sung by Mary Hopkins, 'Knock Knock Who's There?' is the runner up and reaches number 2 in the UK charts.

NIC CULVERWELL: Easy listening pop was the first music I fell in love with. I became a fan of Dana after she won Eurovision and see her as being a very underrated singer despite her relative commercial success.

23rd March – Keith Potger and The New Seekers play Dendy Cinema in Melbourne

Having played three UK venues during February and April, they perform live in Australia, eventually returning to the UK for concerts there later that month.

CHRIS BARRINGTON: Playing Australia was so weird as to start with we'd been playing these working men's clubs in the UK really I guess for us to get 'stage fit'.

To get over there we flew first class, which was great for a teenager in those days. Getting off the plane, we looked across the tarmac and saw a crowd of people. It turned out they were all from the Australian media and there to welcome The New Seekers. Unbeknownst to us, weeks before we arrived, David Joseph had instigated a blitz of publicity across Australia.

Consequently on arriving in Australia we were already well known. That tour was fantastic!

SALLY GRAHAM: With Australia being such an enormous country of course we had to fly everywhere over there.

After that first flight we were subsequently told we had to stay on the plane until everybody else had gotten off, anticipating crowds of journalists with flash bulbs waiting on the tarmac. However, one time we were practically kicked off the plane, even though we were adamant that we had to stay on, as an important politician was visiting and no one at all was waiting for us.

Whilst we stayed in nice hotels, at the same time we weren't allowed to go out, as we would get mobbed, so we effectively felt like prisoners.

MARTY KRISTIAN: In those early days Keith Potger played an important role in the development of The New Seekers.

CHRIS BARRINGTON: Keith was a good guy, his intentions were honest.

MARTY KRISTIAN: Looking back, I felt at the time he was a very hard task master.

However up to that point I only knew three or four chords so I could play basic rock 'n' roll songs. Keith became a great mentor, teaching me to finger pick and showing me different chord structures. As well as that he taught us harmonies. It was a steep learning curve.

Without Keith Potger's input we wouldn't have gotten anywhere.

KEITH POTGER: I don't think I was cracking the whip or anything [laughing]. No, we had a lot of fun!

27th March, 3ʳᵈ April, 10ᵗʰ April, 17ᵗʰ April, 24ᵗʰ April & the 8ᵗʰ May – *Finders Seekers* is broadcast between 8.30pm to 9pm on Scottish TV

The show is a vehicle for The New Seekers. Whilst it is syndicated internationally, the public do not seem to show much interest in the group from the series.

KEITH POTGER: The Seekers were friends of Scottish Television, so with that we may have received a leg up there. Having a Scottish lass in Eve Graham, apart from the fact they were a good group, may have also helped!

SALLY GRAHAM: Whilst we recorded the TV series we were touring Scotland and staying in this hotel where we rehearsed in the dining room early in the morning, before the guests had breakfast, and then we played live somewhere in the evening.

CHRIS BARRINGTON: Each half hour programme was based around a theme, for instance one time it was 'children's songs' so we sang 'The Ugly Duckling'. It was horrible. We scrambled to get things together for each edition.

SALLY GRAHAM: I remembered one of the songs we performed as being 'Puff The Magic Dragon'.

CHRIS BARRINGTON: Shows weren't scripted, it was all very ad hoc.

SALLY GRAHAM: At that time we used Graham Hall as our arranger, who was terrific at that.
I remember that at that time Graham was married to Rona, the sister of Olivia Newton John, and they both sat in the stalls as part of the audience watching the recording of the show. Bruce Welch of The Shadows was Olivia's boyfriend then. In fact Olivia for a while was my babysitter.

A July 1970 shot of Olivia Newton John as part of the group *Toomorrow* with group members *Vic Cooper to the left of her and Ben Thomas to right. Karl Chambers is also a member of Toomorrow.*

The group was put together by US producer Don Kirschner, who had already been involved with manufactured groups The Monkees and The Archies. Whilst there were two single releases, one of which was produced by Bruce Welch, there was also a film, which, with the central idea being 'dying aliens kidnap the group with their music important for the human race's survival', seems to have been something of a promotional vehicle for the project.

During the time of the TV recording of Finders Keepers *the solo career of Olivia Newton John was around a year away from being properly launched.*

What we were asked to do on the show I found soul destroying. I have a sense Olivia and Rona may have been holding back their laughter whilst watching us.

KEITH POTGER: Whether or not it succeeded with viewing ratings, from my point of view it was another stepping stone on the pathway towards international success.

It's difficult to know whether, if we had lost any stepping stone on that pathway, The New Seekers would have been as much of a success as they turned out to be.

April & May - The New Seekers perform at The Savoy

SALLY GRAHAM: Laurie, Chris and myself started to question why we were doing the project.

For instance, going to a midnight show at The Savoy we'd be holding our microphone stands hailing a taxi as no transport would be laid on for us getting there or coming back.

They told us we were trying to sabotage the act at this performance as we were mucking around a bit, not that any of the audience noticed as we were always very professional.

You'd suddenly realise that you weren't happy and as I was young I started to think it would be better to do something else that I would enjoy more.

21st April to 30th May – Keith Potger and The New Seekers play The London Palladium
The group support UK entertainer Max Bygraves.

SALLY GRAHAM: When we played The Palladium I appeared in the programme twice. I'm part of the picture of The New Seekers and they also used an old photograph of The Go Jos they hadn't updated, the dance group I was part of, who were also on the same bill.

This was something that clearly reflected those days before the internet!

KEITH POTGER: David Mackay was brought in to produce The New Seekers, who had been behind a string of hits in Australia.

Working for EMI in Australia the company felt he should go over to produce acts in the UK. Eventually he broke away from EMI and became an independent producer. A group he was producing called Quartet came over to England.

He was in London so we got in touch with him and had a long chat.

CHRIS BARRINGTON: In my opinion David Joseph tried as hard as he could to give Keith free rein to do what he wanted to do, but as it wasn't working David Mackay came in.

DAVID MACKAY: The New Seekers had been performing across the UK in cabaret. Keith had secured them a record deal with Phillips but their two album releases had achieved no success. Phillips offered them one last single release, which would be do or die.

I went to see them in a club, but it was too 'mums and dads' – extremely old-fashioned, and I couldn't honestly see much potential. I just put them out of my mind, but, two weeks later, I was called by a guy from Polydor who had secured the publishing rights of 'Look What They've Done to My Song Ma', a Melanie Safka tune. He also suggested a girl singer to me, but she was hopeless. She couldn't sing her way out of a paper bag!

I really liked the song, though, and I thought it might actually work for The New Seekers. If done correctly, it would give them a more youthful image. Keith Potger went along with the idea. I recorded it with the band. Phillips weren't happy with it, though. They were sure it wasn't going to work. Fortunately, we owned the international rights. In the end, it was released by Jac Holzman's Electra label in the US.

EVE GRAHAM: I can remember Dave Mackay coming backstage to see me at the London Palladium when no one else was there. He had brought a small record player with him and put on an album. All of a sudden David came to this song. He wanted The New Seekers to perform this one as he believed I could deliver a great vocal. It was Melanie Safka singing 'What Have They Done To My Song Ma'.

SALLY GRAHAM: Keith Potger introduced David to us all and explained what he was going to do and we were all very enthusiastic about him.

CHRIS BARRINGTON: My memory is that David brought in a little keyboard and played 'What Have They Done To My Song Ma'.

EVE GRAHAM: I told David it was a horrible song. I thought it was just dreadful. I didn't understand what the words meant and, because I liked story songs, I thought it was too repetitive.

CHRIS BARRINGTON: David would sit with Keith and play the parts then afterwards we'd rehearse it.

EVE GRAHAM: Of course we recorded 'What Have They Done To My Song Ma' (titled 'Look What They've Done To My Song Ma' for the US market) and it became our first hit.

Since then I have never argued with David about what makes a good song and to this day David Mackay still remains my producer of choice!

KEITH POTGER: David was an affable, wonderful guy who was able to relate very much to the sound of the group as he loved harmonies.

He wrote some fantastic arrangements for The New Seekers.

CHRIS BARRINGTON: Bringing in David Mackay was a great move but by that time Sally, Laurie and myself had just had enough of The New Seekers project.

3rd May – The New Seekers appear on British TV's *The Golden Shot*

This was a hugely popular British Sunday afternoon game show hosted by witty comedian Bob Monkhouse, who was part of the legendary British Carry On team. The Golden Shot was based on the bizarre concept of a contestant, sometimes blindfolded, controlling a crossbow a cameraman held by shouting directions with the objective of the arrow hitting the bullseye of a target so prizes could be won. The character 'Bernie The Bolt' was created as the figure who put the arrow in this imaginary crossbow.

The intermissions in the show presented opportunities for musical and comedy performances.

SALLY GRAHAM: David Joseph came into our rehearsals at St Mark's Church Hall to tell us some news he clearly thought we'd all be excited to hear, which, after a dramatic pause, resulted in him announcing he had secured us a spot on *The Golden Shot*.

Marty, being an Ozzie, didn't know about this show, whilst Chris and Laurie fell about laughing in hysterics, which resulted in David Joseph becoming very annoyed with them.

In our minds we were going through a list that included The Royal Variety Performance, Caesar's Palace or a film, as opposed to *The Golden Shot*.

62

The show was pre-recorded and I was the person who had to describe what was in the picnic hamper prize - however, I was unable to do that as either Laurie or Chris had somehow contrived to lock it!

KEITH POTGER: We were able to secure important TV slots partly due to our booking agents but partly due to The New Seekers being able to deliver as they were good looking, they played their instruments well, they sang beautifully and they were well dressed.

I guess their success in securing important TV slots was a combination of those factors.

10ᵗʰ May – Ironically without any noticeable vocal harmonising, the song 'Back Home', performed by England's football World Cup squad, reaches number 1 in the UK charts

The England football team are about to embark on the defence of their world championship title in Mexico as those 'back home' watch their matches nervously on coloured TV for the first time.

16th May – Keith Potger and The New Seekers appear on the BBC2 TV programme *The Young Generation*

Other guests include Lou Rawls and Nina.

13ᵗʰ June – The Beatles achieve their last number 1 in the US

'The Long and Winding Road' becomes their 20ᵗʰ chart topper there.

14ᵗʰ June - England are no longer football world champions

The team were knocked out of the Mexico World Cup, beaten 3-2 by West Germany, rivals who they had beaten to become world champions in the first place. They did not qualify for another World Cup Finals competition until 1982.

CHAPTER 4
June to December 1970: Renaissance Period - Goodbye Chris, Laurie, and Sally; Hello Lyn, Peter and Paul

19th June – The New Seekers play a summer season at the ABC in the coastal town of Great Yarmouth, UK

The New Seekers have been contracted to undertake a 12 week engagement supporting Herman's Hermits in Holiday Startime, with comedian Ted Rogers also on the bill, who later becomes famous for hosting the popular 80s ITV variety quiz show 321 in Britain, which includes the character 'Dusty Bin'.

SALLY GRAHAM: The chemistry between the five of us in that first line up when we performed live was great. We certainly delivered a great show!

Of course away from that live context it was very different, with the three of us being so close and not taking the project quite as seriously as the other two (Marty and Eve).

Sometime during that period there appears to be a seamless, Doctor Who-like changeover from The New Seekers mark one line up to the mark two line up, as Lyn Paul replaces Sally Graham, and Peter Doyle and Paul Layton replace Laurie and Chris respectively. Apart from Paul Layton's audition, the impression given to me is that Lyn and Peter Doyle were chosen without audition.

KEITH POTGER: Rather than the line up changeover taking place during a fallow period for the group, we were fortunate that we already had that summer season booked, which made the transition much smoother.

CHRIS BARRINGTON: 'The straw that broke the camel's back' for Sally, Laurie and myself was that 12 week booking in Great Yarmouth, which we just didn't want to do!

It would have been a tremendous grind, performing material that we were just not interested in.

KEITH POTGER: We already had Paul, Peter and Lyn in place, ready to go. The whole transition was well thought through.

MARTY KRISTIAN: I had walked out on the group and the only reason I stayed was that David Joseph told me Peter Doyle was joining.

SALLY GRAHAM: They knew we weren't happy by the time of the Great Yarmouth booking, so they had decided the three of us were going to leave and had put plan B in place, with three people already lined up to take over!

We would have stuck it out to the end. In my opinion it was a management decision they made long before we knew it was going to happen.

I have a vague recollection (but can't be sure) that we didn't know about the changeover before the Great Yarmouth booking, as if we had been told we might well not have helped the new line up with the rehearsals and changeover.

CHRIS BARRINGTON: We sat with our respective partner, in my case Paul Layton, during the day in our room, teaching that person their part. We were quite happy to do that. There was no animosity there at all.

SALLY GRAHAM: We were staying in a hotel where there was enough room there to teach the people coming in the material for our set. I remember being given a directive by David Joseph not to mix with them socially.

My memory was we were all together in a conference room with each other rehearsing.

CHRIS BARRINGTON: Laurie and I knew Paul from school. I remember him being kinda goofy but really likeable all the same. He drove a Dodge Dart which was most impressive!

I was surprised when I heard Paul was coming into the group, simply because I knew him and it was so unexpected. However I was pleased for Paul that he wanted to become a New Seeker. It was a great opportunity for him.

KEITH POTGER: To their credit Sally, Laurie and Chris were very professional about the whole changeover. The whole process was very agreeable.

CHRIS BARRINGTON: It was a great way to finish The New Seekers project.

My passion was never music, but I was a good actor, so maybe I should have gone to RADA instead; but there again acting didn't turn out to be my passion either.

MARTY KRISTIAN: With that first line up there were all sorts of issues with contracts.

CHRIS BARRINGTON: I previously had contracts with agents for the acting work I had been doing before The New Seekers, yet somehow on joining The New Seekers, without my knowledge and behind the scenes, David Joseph bought out my contract.

MARTY KRISTIAN: There were relationship problems between members of the group and there were money problems so they all decided to leave.

CHRIS BARRINGTON: David Joseph was exceptionally money orientated and in my opinion purely put the group together so that it could make him a lot of money.

Members in the group earned very little money from The New Seekers.

PAUL LAYTON: My understanding was Laurie, Chris and Sally left because they decided it was time to move on. Laurie I think was writing songs and they wanted to go in a different direction.

They wanted to express themselves musically, whereas with The New Seekers being manufactured they had to follow a set format, which they weren't comfortable to do.

CHRIS BARRINGTON: The three of us decided we should leave and do something together on our own because we didn't enjoy what we were doing and because we felt we weren't getting paid enough for doing it.

PAUL LAYTON: Keith tried to put something together that was going to be a progression on from The Seekers, albeit a little less folky.

CHRIS BARRINGTON: David Joseph was generally friendly most of the time; however, I remember Laurie Heath engaging in a huge argument when we were rehearsing one time where they almost came to blows about something.

Both Laurie and David had forceful characters so they clashed.

PAUL LAYTON: I also believe Laurie, Chris and Sally were disenchanted with the management, and the payment they were receiving, whereas our version just knuckled down and got on with it.

KEITH POTGER: From my recollection Sally, Laurie and Chris left the group because they were unhappy with the repertoire they were being asked to perform.

CHRIS BARRINGTON: It was Laurie's idea that the three of us should leave and form our own band which would be more traditionally folk in nature.

KEITH POTGER: I don't remember their departure being due to any contractual issue and if so that financial side would have been easier to resolve. With there being a cultural difference on both sides over the repertoire, effectively they felt they had to grit their teeth to perform.

Unlike the subsequent line up, where it felt like we were all pulling in the same direction, with those three members in the first line up there was a divergence over the direction the repertoire should go in.

At the original audition we took what Laurie, Chris and Sally said on face value and hoped they took our ideas on the group on face value too. Perhaps in the end what they were letting themselves in for was not quite what they had in mind. Although they committed themselves to the group for well over a year I believe they gradually realised The New Seekers project was not quite what they expected it to be.

CHRIS BARRINGTON: The three of us didn't like what we were being given to do, that was the main reason we left.

PAUL LAYTON: The set up with the group was described to me by Marty, the deal was modest and we were paid a retainer wage with costumes and instrumentation covered by the management company.

We all signed contracts and moved forward from there.

Later on we had some issues with the contracts but we re-negotiated and got separate representations, which improved the situation a little bit.

We were rehearsed intensely by Keith over a couple of months. The format of the group was five individuals each making an input from a varied talent base so chemistry could develop, with each person bringing something unique to the party.

DAVID MACKAY (Producer): Peter Doyle had a voice to die for. He was just an amazing singer.

SALLY GRAHAM: With that second line up of The New Seekers after the three of us left I always listened out for the voice of Peter Doyle. He had the most amazing voice.

MARTY KRISTIAN: David Joseph persuaded me to stay as he said Peter Doyle was joining the group. I knew what a great talent Peter was, working with him on *The Go!! Show*.

With Peter joining it was going to result in something good and in the end he became an integral part of the group.

KEITH POTGER: David Joseph knew Peter Doyle better than I did, although I knew of his reputation.

Peter was in the UK as The Virgil Brothers had broken up. He was a really fine guitarist as well as being a tremendous singer.

PAUL LAYTON: I didn't know Keith Potger and David Joseph at all. I auditioned at The London Palladium in front of Keith. It was some time after that I met David. Effectively Keith made the decision musically about me. I think my acting experience stood me in good stead for taking on roles in the act so that must have played a part. For example we did an Oliver medley and I played Fagin.

MARTY KRISTIAN: Peter Doyle was a tremendous talent in his own right. In those early days, when we were being worked hard and having to keep to a strict regime, as he was by nature something of a loose cannon; I think that regime was good for him as Peter had an order in his life. I remember those very early days when we played songs together very fondly.

I had met Paul Layton in the UK through us having a shared Ossie Byrne connection so he was already a friend.

I was kept informed about the change of personnel and for me it was just the right time for that first version of the band to disintegrate when it did.

With Eve and Lyn already having sung together in The Nocturnes, both singers recognise in recordings their voices blend together superbly well, creating sonic magic.

EVE GRAHAM: When I knew Sally was leaving I told Keith and David to bring Lyn in as I just knew it would work.

KEITH POTGER: My memory is that Lyn got involved in The New Seekers due to Eve's recommendation through their partnership singing in The Nocturnes together. She was the best candidate and seamlessly stepped in.

From memory the relationship between Lyn and Eve was like one within a close knit family, with very little age difference between the two of them.

PAUL DRAYTON: Ossie Byrne had to release me, but he thought joining The New Seekers would be good for my career. In knowing me Marty also put some good words in on my behalf. By that stage we were friends that socialised and played music together. Marty was most definitely in my corner when I came to audition.

EVE GRAHAM: They gave Lyn another chance and of course once we got going it was dynamite with the two of us! We sang together and were great foils for each other. I always felt there was tremendous chemistry between the two of us. I enjoyed working with her and I enjoyed working with Sandra [Stevens who would later become a mainstay in hit vocal pop group The Brotherhood of Man] as well in The Nocturnes but I always felt Lyn was a much stronger singer than Sandra. Also Lyn's personality was much more in balance with mine; there was a definite yin and yang.

DAVID MACKAY: Lyn and Eve together had a magical sound. When you think of Abba, it was based on that sort of template with those female harmonies.

PAUL LAYTON: To start with I had the idea I would audition for The New Seekers as a guitarist but when they told me that Peter Doyle had already got that role and they needed a bass player I blagged that I could do that (which of course I couldn't).

When they found out I'd never played the bass before it was agreed I would be given a short period of time to prove I could play the bass. Thanks to Ossie Byrne, who rang his bassist friends, I used someone's bass and learnt the parts on the first New Seekers album. When I went back, although I wasn't singing anything at the time, they were suitably impressed that I was playing bass whilst the others sang. I got the job!

SALLY GRAHAM: The Seekers were an acoustic group with Athol Guy even playing the double bass.

Chris Barrington and then Paul Layton playing the electric bass represented quite a departure from that Seekers musical template.

EVE GRAHAM: I remember the changeover of personnel as we rehearsed every afternoon with Peter, Paul and Lyn, who were to be in the new line up. They did everything word for word in the same way Chris, Sally and Laurie had done. They followed the same dance steps and routines by watching the evening performances.

PAUL LAYTON: With Peter and Lyn I rehearsed the show in a hotel room during the day and then we went to see their show in the evening. It was scheduled that the changeover would take place one Saturday evening into that Great Yarmouth engagement.

Michael Grade, who is probably most famous for being controller of the BBC, had by this stage left a career in journalism and moved into his father's theatrical business representing artists.

EVE GRAHAM: Michael Grade was told three out of the five members were being replaced and was horrified. Michael came down to watch a rehearsal and changed his mind, accepting the audience wouldn't know the difference.

SALLY GRAHAM: Reflecting back now, if I stayed on with Chris Barrington and Peter Doyle came in with Eve and Marty already there, that chemistry of personalities would have been fantastic.

EVE GRAHAM: Suddenly there was a new line up on stage that were doing the same things as the old line up were, which is what I remember most about the line up change over. It was all very clever.

SALLY GRAHAM: I remember saying goodbye to Peter Noone (lead singer of the headliners Herman's Hermits, who we were supporting), who was surprised about the change over and actually quite annoyed no one had told him.
The night after we left, our photographs had been taken down and I couldn't even get a complimentary ticket to see the new line up's first performance.
We were told not to tell anyone why we left. Having got hold of my number, someone from the *Daily Express* rang me and asked me that question. My reply was tongue in cheek as I said 'I couldn't afford to do it any longer!' which was a line that was published.

PAUL LAYTON: That first performance was frightening.

We were in a big theatre with a pit orchestra. I arrived on stage locking in with a drummer I had never met so I remember the look of horror on his face as he had no idea the line up was going to change. All the dancers on the show were staring out from the wings agog. We literally did the job the three outgoing members of the group had been doing previously.

My recollection was that I was so nervous my top lip stuck to my tongue and when I smiled I couldn't release it! It was a great challenge but it only lasted for 25 minutes.

EVE GRAHAM: When Lyn first joined The New Seekers she had this pixie cut, which at the time was really fashionable, but they wanted two female singers with long hair so unfortunately she had to wear a wig until her hair grew underneath it.

KEITH POTGER: I took on a different role with Eve, Lyn, Paul, Peter and Marty depending on the context. When we were in rehearsal mode it was a case of being a teacher; however, in a more relaxed atmosphere I might have been more of a big brother to each of them.

I was always in awe of each individual regarding how they approached their particular position in the group.

For instance, although Eve often contributed lead vocals, Lyn was still very professional with how she fitted in, though of course she eventually took on those lead vocals tremendously well with those later hits.

Marty was always very professional too but it was Paul who was always the super reliable one. He always seemed to take on this backstop role with anything that needed to be done.

PAUL LAYTON: Keith worked us very hard. Playing sometimes six days a week, we got to know each other very quickly.

EVE GRAHAM: They were working us very hard and although I never really followed what they did after The New Seekers I got the impression the three that left that first line up went in more of a folk direction.

They didn't change; it was The New Seekers that changed as we all became more poppy and part of something much bigger.

SALLY GRAHAM: With Peter Doyle joining, The New Seekers became more of a pop group.

They wouldn't have become commercially successful without Peter, he gave The New Seekers that edge.

71

KEITH POTGER: You don't set up a business with the idea you expect it to fail.

When we changed the line up, David Joseph and I both felt everyone was pulling in the same direction.

SALLY GRAHAM: Before we left The New Seekers, Laurie, Chris and myself had already made plans, booking a studio and getting some musicians in to record songs.

At one stage we even met with Derek Taylor, who was the publicist for The Beatles.

KEITH POTGER: With that second line up of The New Seekers, individual members in the group, the management, producer Dave Mackay and our agency all became a tight team. It was a joint effort for a long, long time - much longer than most groups could sustain.

SALLY GRAHAM: Although I had become unhappy with the project, overviewing my time as a New Seeker it was good fun!

CHRIS BARRINGTON: Laurie Heath knew Ossie Byrne, who suggested that the three of us go to Tony De Fries for some legal advice with what had just happened to us with The New Seekers. At that time Tony was looking after Bowie.

A shot of Tony De Fries next to David Bowie in 1971

SALLY GRAHAM: We used to regularly visit Tony De Fries in Maida Vale, who in the end decided that he couldn't help us legally. We'd have this big meal there with people like David Bowie, at the time when he was married to Angie.

CHRIS BARRINGTON: At one stage we played in front of Bowie's backing band when he was working on *Hunky Dory*. Mick Ronson was lovely and became a good friend of mine.

SALLY GRAHAM: After my intense experience in The New Seekers I didn't see Eve, Marty or Paul ever again.
   I guess, looking back, I assumed I would have stayed in touch with Eve with what we had gone through together. Although there was such strong chemistry between myself, Laurie and Chris, I always got along well with Eve.
   Directly after The New Seekers I sold my flat in London and bought a house, which I refurbished.

21st June – Brazil become football champions of the world for the third time

With Brazil taking the world championship mantle from England as they beat Italy 4-1 this became the first football World Cup final broadcast to the world in colour.

Fittingly the Brazil side play dazzling football in eye-catching colours of gold and blue. For some people this Brazil side is regarded as the best football team of all time.

The scoring is rounded off by one of the best goals of all time as the Brazil captain Carlos Alberto ends a flowing move with a powerful shot which ends up in the corner of the net.

30th July – The New Seekers' debut on *Top Of The Pops* is broadcast

In an edition hosted by Jimmy Savile, the popular Radio One DJ of the time, the new line up performed 'What Have They Done To My Song Ma' several months before the single was released. Unfortunately the recording of this edition has been lost; however, the group apparently were in awe of Aretha Franklin, who performed her top 20 UK hit 'Don't Play That Song'. Hotlegs were on the show performing their hit single 'Neanderthal Man'. They were later to become 10cc.

The programme was a TV sensation in the UK.

CHRIS BARRINGTON: I shared this strange British sense of humour with Laurie and Sally, which I guess we didn't share with Eve and Marty. Sometimes we'd be laughing at things and neither Marty or Eve understood what it was we were laughing at. We were fans of Monty Python.

We just about got through the recording of 'What Have They Done To My Song Ma' but I have to say we were laughing so hard at that session.

PAUL LAYTON: Strangely, before I joined The New Seekers I was with Ossie Byrne when David Joseph brought the vinyl of 'What Have They Done To My Song Ma' over that the original line up played on. I thought it was fantastic and could see it had the potential of becoming a huge hit.

Of course soon after this I ended up promoting that record, which I didn't perform on, as a fully fledged New Seeker.

15th August – The New Seekers appear on London Weekend Television show *Maggie's Place*

DAVID MACKAY: Paul Layton played the bass as well as sang the bass parts. It was a great combination amongst the five of them. They were good learners and were keen to get on with the work they were given without questioning anything. We went on tour together and I never heard a cross word between them.

On my watch there was never any arguing between any of them.

14th September – The first colour broadcast of *Blue Peter* **takes place**

At that time Blue Peter *was a popular children's BBC1 TV magazine show with Valerie Singleton, John Noakes and Peter Purves as regular presenters.*

15th September – The popular TV programme *Skippy: The Bush Kangaroo* **debuts on British TV**

Described as an Australian Flipper or Lassie it is based around a young boy having adventures through his relationship with a tame kangaroo who he feels he can communicate with. Filmed at (what is now) Waratah Park in North Sydney, for many British children, myself included, it will be their first 'real' experience of Australia, albeit through the medium of television.

NIC CULVERWELL: In the UK at that time you only ever went to Australia if you were emigrating there.

17th October – With David Mackay this time producing, released on Phillips, the single 'What Have They Done To My Song Ma' reaches the UK top 50

Ironically with Eve as the lead vocalist, this single release, which became the group's first hit, was recorded by the first line up. Sometime during the single's UK chart run The New Seekers, with the second line up, make their first appearance on BBC1's Top of the Pops, *a television sensation in the UK.*

The single will become a (retitled) top 20 hit in the US whilst in Australia and Canada the single reaches number three and number two respectively in the charts.

75

EVE GRAHAM: With David's arrangement the song was smooth pop, whereas Melanie's version [Melanie Safka's original] had that distinctive rough vocal. He always thought the most difficult thing for a producer to do was to spend two days getting the flute parts right only to cut them out altogether in the final mix. He would do big orchestrations but he had a feel for what made a good pop record.

DAVID MACKAY: At EMI my office was next to Norman 'Hurricane' Smith who engineered the early Beatles records. He was a great guy and a great musician, particularly in playing the saxophone. I learned so much from him as he was such a fabulous engineer and producer. The year I was at Abbey Road was such an incredible learning curve and experience for me. For instance I remember Tim Rice and Andrew Lloyd Webber coming into the office at 5pm, just as we were off to the pub, telling us they were working on the *Jesus Christ Superstar* musical.

Being an Australian producer, my objective at Abbey Road Studios was to bring Australian artists to the UK and promote them. I tried to get the company interested in Johnny Farnham, who became enormously successful in Australia and of course had a huge international hit in the 80s with 'You're The Voice', but they didn't want to know, feeling they already had Cliff Richard. I produced a group called The Wallace Collection that became successful across Europe, USA and Canada. However, the company wasn't supporting the group's record releases with promotion in the UK. In fact they weren't releasing a lot of the stuff I had produced. I felt I was faced with the choice of going back to Australia or giving it a crack on my own. As I wasn't getting records out I decided it was pointless renewing my contract with EMI and with only five hundred pounds to my name, rented a flat with two Australian friends, and set up June Productions Limited.

Fortunately 'What Have They Done To My Song Ma' was an early success for me when I went independent.

KEITH POTGER: David Mackay had been sitting on his ideas for this Melanie Safka song and in Eve's voice he found the perfect vehicle through which he was able to deliver those ideas. His production of the song marked the beginning of a long lasting friendship between David and the group.

Although I arranged and produced the first album David had a lot more experience with this area than I had. David was a very good musician as well as being a producer and arranger. I felt my skills lay more on the musician side of things in the team. My producing experience in The Seekers had been alongside Tom Springfield but David was comfortable producing on his own so in that sense he had all that we needed him to have in that direction.

Bringing David on board as a producer was like putting on board a pair of warm slippers. Quartet, the group he was producing when he first came on board, ended up playing on many of those New Seeker tracks. I was very happy to be a side man for David Mackay, occasionally contributing guitar.

PAUL LAYTON: David was hugely important to The New Seekers. He was a very musical person and had great schooling behind him. He used to score orchestral parts and had a great ear. He loved melody and was just what the group needed at the time.

25th October – The New Seekers appear on *The Ed Sullivan Show* in the US, the programme that arguably broke The Beatles in that country, performing 'Look What They've Done To My Song Ma', which is released on Elektra, but interestingly with the title wording different from the Melanie Safka original and the UK release. As well as this the release gives a 'featuring' credit for lead vocalist Eve Graham

On the show, celebrating the 25th Anniversary of The United Nations, guest performers from around the world are featured including Astrud Gilberto representing Brazil and Ravi Shankar representing India. The New Seekers are billed as representing Australia, which must have felt strange for Eve, Lyn and Paul.

MARTY KRISTIAN: Whilst we were performing in the UK we heard the single had reached the top 40 in the US. Myself and Peter Doyle especially knew that this was a tremendous accolade. I believe the success of the song enabled us to tour the US and David Joseph was able to book us onto various TV shows over there.

PAUL LAYTON: It was a great experience appearing on *Ed Sullivan*. We were eventually photographed with him outside the theatre. When we were introduced by Ed as coming from Australia that was the first time I knew that was going to happen!

MARTY KRISTIAN: I remember asking Ravi Shankar how long it had taken him to master the sitar and of course he replied 'My son, one never masters one's instrument - one is always learning'

77

31st October – 'Look What They've Done To My Song Ma' by The New Seekers featuring Eve Graham reaches a US Billboard chart peak of 14

DAVID MACKAY: When I listened to the original by Melanie Safka she put across the song in a very straightforward, correct way. Effectively I destroyed the song in the middle part and made it sound hideous, creating this 'look what you've done to my song, you've ruined it' effect before the song goes back into a very joyous feel. I guess you might say I took a very theatrical approach towards the song. You try to work with the song and make your presentation of it unique.

SALLY GRAHAM: Keith Potger by his own admission wasn't really a producer even though he'd taken on that role for the first album.
Dave Mackay on the other hand was a professional producer changing the dynamics of the whole thing. He was also a really nice bloke!
The recording was good fun.

CHRIS BARRINGTON: David reconstructed that song. It was clear he knew what he was doing. We were given our parts and delivered them. Laurie, Sally and I enjoyed that session. We all knew that what David had captured was really good.

PAUL LAYTON: A record is a combination of things. It's the vocal performance, the arrangement and of course also the song. 'Look What They've Done' had this unique musical solo interlude that David had created with the squeaky violin and it just worked. We didn't have a violin on stage but we made some silly vocal noises, banged into a key change and then it took off. It was a fantastic vocal performance there from Eve.

EVE GRAHAM: It was a hit in the US as David Joseph went to thirteen record companies hoping that one would pick it up and of course Elektra did. With the next single the radio stations flipped the B side and played 'Beautiful People'. Rather than having two female singers sharing vocals, for a while there was an insistence on my taking the lead vocal as it was felt 'if it ain't broke why fix it'.

KEITH POTGER: We had signed to Elektra in the US as David Joseph hit it off really well with Jac Holzman, who was head of the label. Jac wanted to expand the market reach of the label. Having The Doors, they were certainly bringing in money, and he figured that The New Seekers were the act that they could do that with. They put quite a bit of finance

78

behind the group with promotion and of course it was all vindicated with 'Look What They've Done To My Song Ma' becoming a big US hit single.

November – The second album of material from the first line up is released with the group credited this time as 'Keith Potger and The New Seekers'. Nevertheless it is the group's recently formed second line up that is shown on the front cover photograph

The photograph for the front cover, under the pier at Great Yarmouth, is taken during that New Seekers summer season, with the bearded Keith Potger on the far right of the picture, when the mark two version of the group was introduced there. All of the group, in a relaxed manner, are wearing casual clothes of the time and there is a noticeable sense of informality, with Eve crouching down next to her dog. There is some debate as to whether this shot was taken before, on or after the day the group changed over.

With two Keith Potger co-writes and a Laurie Heath original, the other nine songs are interpretations. Whilst Keith is credited for producing two tracks, with Peter Roberts producing one, nine tracks are now produced by David Mackay. The orchestral arrangements are undertaken by Bill Shepherd and Johnny Arthey rather than by Keith. The name of The New Seekers' management company has now changed to Toby Artistes Management Ltd.

A FAN'S PERSPECTIVE ON THE ALBUM: You could perhaps retitle this release 'The Under The Pier Album'. Those buying it might not have realised that the tracks were performed by the first line up and not the second line up photographed on the cover. They might also not have realised the shot was taken during the time the mark one line up became mark two, when the group were playing a summer season in Great Yarmouth. It does include the recording of their first hit (in North America and Australia as opposed to the UK). There is debate as to when exactly it is shot but, with the group certainly as a unit hardly knowing each other, it is amazing that chemistry is shown to be there already with that picture.

Comparing it with the first release, there is a very different style of songs chosen on this album in that they are perhaps more current, with Beatles, Paul Simon and Melanie Safka interpretations. 'All Right My Love' is recognised by fans as a New Seekers classic with an Eve Graham lead vocal. All of the songs are very good. The group's version of 'Here, There and Everywhere' has Keith Potger on lead vocals; later the song is revisited with Lyn Paul on lead vocals. The song on the album 'I'm A Train' was apparently the first song Lyn, Peter and Paul learnt with the group and that

79

song, along with 'Mrs Robinson', remained in the group's live act for quite some time.

EVE GRAHAM: I just remember that one picture being taken for the cover and my little dog being in that shot. You could say there was this change in image but to be honest I was just going with the flow.

I loved The New Seekers from the beginning because of the harmonies. With the change of personnel, to me the songs just seemed more bouncy. There seemed to be a lot more life in the whole thing. We were growing, that's all.

SALLY GRAHAM: Looking at that cover, having by now left the group, I wondered what was going on.

Although the line up I was part of sang the material that was on that album it seemed to suggest everything had changed with the casual look of the group. It leaves me questioning: 'How come it all changed?'

I honestly think the management was making it up as they went along and there was no master plan or formula.

EVE GRAHAM: The idea of Keith being part of the group was just to get the whole thing going as he was the famous one. He intended to back off once the whole thing took off. Keith didn't want to keep touring and instead wanted to take more of a management role in the background.

PAUL LAYTON: The photograph, showing Eve's dog, Pepsi, was taken in Great Yarmouth, I think before the changeover. It was a casual look and very different to what we were doing on stage, which was more formal. For instance the boys wore beige suits and the girls wore long dresses.

That image on the cover shot was more reflective of how our style would change and it became more individual when we toured the US.

CHRIS BARRINGTON: In my opinion the production values on this album with David on board were of an infinitely higher quality than the first album. He was focused, knew what he wanted and got what he wanted.

8ᵗʰ November – The first ever episode of the cult comedy show *The Goodies* is aired on BBC2
With BBC1 overshadowing this channel so comprehensively in those days even before video recorders it could be said at the time 'the only

reason to watch BBC2 is so that I can see The Goodies*'. It was a hugely popular series amongst the young popular music listeners in Britain.*

The series' basic structure revolved around the trio, always short of money, offering themselves for hire – with the tagline 'We Do Anything, Anytime, Anywhere' – to perform all sorts of ridiculous but generally benevolent tasks. The musical Bill Oddie played the hippy character with Graeme Garden the intellectual and Tim Brooke-Taylor a conservative man of principles. With each episode based around a story containing surrealistic comedy, it was in many ways a much looser, more populist version of Monty Python.

The series continues at BBC2 until 1980 and after that it is broadcast across at London Weekend Television for ITV.

15th November – The New Seekers appear on *The Golden Shot*
This is their second appearance on the show.

NIC CULVERWELL: Although we only had three-channel TV in Britain back in those days they actually serviced the music industry very well. Variety was important, particularly on BBC. The major stars of the day had their own shows where they had big name guests on.

9th December – Keith Potger and The New Seekers appear on TV show *Lift Off with Ayshea*
Lift Off with Ayshea *(first called* Lift Off*) was a British TV show produced by Granada Television, starring Ayshea Brough, which ran for 122 editions between November 1969 and December 1974. Ayshea was one of the first women of Asian heritage to present a British television series.*

The premise of the show was to showcase music requested by viewers writing into the series. The requests were interspersed with performances of either new releases or current hits. Generally only two or three guest acts would appear each week with the majority of the songs performed by Ayshea herself.

13ᵗʰ December – The New Seekers appear on a second *Ed Sullivan Show*, performing a medley which includes 'Look What They've Done To My Song Ma', 'Your Song', 'Baby Face' and 'Beautiful People'
Also appearing were Les Ballets Africains, comedian Guy Marks, Merrill (baritone singer from The Met), impressionist Marilyn Michaels

81

(who sang 'Swanee' as a tribute to Judy Garland), cast members from the Broadway production of The Rothschilds, Bobby Sherman (who sang 'Going Home' and 'Song Of Joy') and Ali MacGraw, the female lead in the hit 1970 film Love Story, *who recited a poem.*

31st December – The Beatles cease to exist
Paul McCartney sues the other members of the group and the group is effectively dissolved.

'In The Summertime' by Mungo Jerry was the best selling single of 1970 in the UK, a song that is very much close to the heart of Mick Flinn, who will become a New Seeker in the next decade!

Chapter 5
1971: The Sweet Smell Of Success - The New Seekers Break Big In The UK

IN THE UK IN 1971...
Divorces exceed 100,000 for the first time * Unemployment reaches a post war high of 815,000 * *The Daily Mail* **is relaunched as a tabloid * Education Secretary Margaret Thatcher decides children should no longer have free school milk * Serious minded TV music show** *The Old Grey Whistle Test* **airs on BBC2 for the very first time * The death toll in The Troubles of Northern Ireland reaches 100**

1ˢᵗ January – *Look-In* **magazine is launched in the UK with a photograph of popular ITV** *Magpie* **presenter Tony Bastable on the front cover.**

Promoted as the junior TV Times (the TV Times was a programme listing magazine focusing more on ITV whilst the Radio Times was a programme listing magazine focusing more on the BBC, along with radio shows... all unnecessarily complicated and British) and aimed at the young teenager market, it is something of a 70s phenomenon. Usually with a hand drawn front cover of a pop star, it contained posters and features on music as well as cartoon strips on TV shows popular with young people. Not as cool as the music inkies, such as the NME, it focused more on mainstream pop.

Magpie was seen as ITV's version of Blue Peter. Incidentally the cool 'One For Sorrow' theme song was written by Eddie Hardin and performed by The Spencer Davis Group under the alias of The Murgatroyd Band.

DONNA JONES: Christine Lowe, who sang in the Chrys Do Lyns, had been staying with myself and my family, as sadly her mum had recently died.

Whilst The New Seekers were starting to make progress Lyn and Eve were sharing a flat together in Streatham, London. Lyn rang Christine inviting her to stay in a room they had free, which she accepted. Unfortunately whilst Lyn and Eve were away there was a fire in the flat with Christine needing to be rescued by the fire service from the attic. After that fire Christine stayed in a flat with Carol, the girlfriend of Marty Kristian (Carol and Marty later married in 1975). Sometime afterwards I moved in there too as my singing career grew and I needed a base in London. Lyn often visited so the three of us would have a good old chinwag about things!

Not long after that Christine moved to London and, using the name Jill Webster, became secretary of The New Seekers fan club until the band disbanded in 1974.

9th January – The New Seekers appear on NBC's *Andy Williams Show*

Along with the song 'One' with Andy Williams, the group performed 'When There's No Love Left', which was released at the back end of last year with 'Beautiful People', although it met with no significant commercial success. The males are dressed in formal Beatles style suits whilst Lyn and Eve are 'a little nun-like' in yellow blouses and brown waistcoats.

The lyrics of the song, with the candles on the set, evoke a Sunday 'Songs Of Praise' atmosphere.

Clearly this is a group still in a transition period.

16th January – The New Seekers appear on the UK BBC1 TV show *It's Cliff* performing 'There's A Light'

On this show Clodagh Rodgers, a singer from Northern Ireland who has been chosen to represent the UK in the 1971 Eurovision Song Contest, sings one of the songs selected for the public vote which will determine which song goes forward to represent the UK at the song contest final in April.

During this second series Cliff introduces Elton John to the great British viewing public, who is in the midst of experiencing his first ever hit single with the ballad 'Your Song', and the 22-year-old Olivia Newton John, who at this time, as a British-born Australian, has something of a girl-next-door image singing what you might term 'light, country pop'. Having released her first single as a teenager in 1966, which does not chart, she performs a cover of the Bob Dylan song written for his wife Sara, 'If Not You', with a George Harrison version having already appeared on his commercially successful album All Things Must Pass. *It became the first hit single for Olivia Newton John, reaching the top ten in both the UK and Australia. My question at this time was: is she British or is she Australian? Cliff had apparently got to know Olivia as she was the then girlfriend of Bruce Welch, one of The Shadows. Of course Olivia goes on to become an Australian icon.*

The talented 24-year-old black British singer-songwriter Labi Siffre is also introduced to the great British public during this series. He goes on to experience hit singles which include 'It Must Be Love', later covered by the British pop group Madness with their version reaching number 4 in the UK charts.

PAUL LAYTON: We had a very professional relationship with Cliff and of course that show gave us tremendous exposure. It suited us as it was a variety show with sketches. For instance, I performed a small cameo, with Eve playing Napoleon, which was later brought into our act. The boys would do a song with Cliff and then the whole group would do a song with Cliff. It majorly increased our fan base.

31st January – 'The Pushbike Song' by Australian group The Mixtures rises to number 2 in the UK charts behind 'My Sweet Lord' by George Harrison
Future New Seeker Mick Flinn, with his previous group The Wild Colonials having dissolved, has by now joined this group as they become a five piece. Taking advantage of the Australian radio ban, which lasts from May to October, where Australian and UK artists on the six largest record labels represented by The Australasian Performing Rights Association (APRA) were refused airplay, the group's cover of Mungo Jerry's 'In The Summertime' has already become a number 1 hit single in Australia, released on Ron Tudor's Fable Records.

Both these records are produced by David Mackay, who very soon becomes the 'go to' producer for The New Seekers.

MICK FLINN: As radio stations in Australia were playing records without paying performing rights to the musicians, which they had felt was perfectly fair as by playing the records they were in effect promoting the songs, for a time during 1970 the big labels through APRA, which often consisted of overseas acts, did not allow radio stations to play their records until the radio stations agreed to pay artists the money they were due.

With Fable Records, Ron Tudor came up with the idea of establishing an Australian roster of groups playing covers of hits and releasing those recordings as singles. He agreed with the radio stations that, without any expectation of being paid by them, they could play these single releases in opposition to this ban. Being one of the Melbourne bands he found to co-operate with, he gave The Mixtures several songs to consider covering, one of which was Mungo Jerry's 'In The Summertime'.

Our lead singer Idris Jones didn't feel it suited his voice so I sang lead vocals on that song. Straight after making our recording of 'In The Summertime' Ron Tudor told us to take it across to the radio stations. Strangely I heard it being played on the radio as I was travelling back home.

With the song eventually achieving number one in Australia I remember going into Ron's office and asking him whether we could get a bit of money for it. I remember his reply was 'You want money as well! You're on TV, you're in the newspapers and you're number one in charts but you want money as well!' He was put out by the request but in the end stated 'I'll have to see what I can do!'

Our producer David Mackay was a very up kinda guy but wasn't keen on 'The Pushbike Song' being released as our next single.

Idris Jones, our lead singer, and his brother Evan wrote the song with it first of all being heavily influenced sound-wise by The Hollies' single 'On A Carousel', especially lyrically with the line that started with the words 'riding along'. One day when we were looking for songs I asked someone to play the song slowed down as I thumped my guitar case and as I was driving along the song 'Neanderthal Man' came into my mind, which I loved, with that thudding percussion. The idea of the shushing hi hat and thudding bass drum came into my mind, which eventually became a great rhythm that was turned into those cycling sound effects in the record. Taping this new version, which included omitting the middle section of the original version, when David Mackay heard this he was adamant we shouldn't release it as he strongly felt it was a rip off of 'In The Summertime'.

Fortunately, as Ron Tudor was behind us recording it, David reluctantly agreed to us doing that but we were only allowed to do one take.

Whilst we were on tour opening in Australia for 1910 Fruitgum Company, most famous for their smash hit song 'Simon Says' (based on the children's movement game 'Simple Simon'), the audience reaction to the song was strong and we told them it would be our next single. However Ron Tudor had already decided our next single would be 'Love Is Life', written by Errol Brown and Tony Wilson [both are members of the band Hot Chocolate and in fact the song is released by that band becoming their first top 10 hit in the UK]. Meeting with Ron, we insisted 'The Pushbike Song' was released because of the reaction to it we had received live and that is what happened. [Ironically 'Love Is Life' was released by The Mixtures in 1974 after Mick had left the band. It was not a hit though.]

Although we had to fight against our producer, Dave Mackay, I'd like to think somewhere in the back of his mind he also thought it could be a hit and felt the song should be recorded so we could get it out there.

February to April – The New Seekers tour the US

Apparently staying at the very best hotels, the group consolidated their success in America by undertaking a full scale concert and cabaret tour. By all accounts these five young adults are treated royally, with, remember, Peter Doyle and Lyn Paul both still in their early twenties.

The New Seekers travel to Florida, Iowa, Illinois and Mississippi. They perform at notable venues such as the Marco Polo Lounge in Miami, The Troubadour in Los Angeles, where on performing there Elton John is arguably broken in the US, and The Bitter End in New York.

PAUL LAYTON: These were the venues to be seen at.

It was not so much a tour, more of a trip. We were spoiled rotten staying at the Plaza in New York and The Beverly Hills Hotel in LA. We travelled on 747s with each of us having a whole row of seats to ourselves.

David Joseph had taken 'What Have They Done To My Song Ma' round to lots of US record companies to get a release but ultimately it was picked up by Jac Holzman of Elektra records, the company I had signed with for my solo career. At one of our gigs I met with Jac, who expressed surprise to see me in this musical incarnation.

I loved harmonising although I was a bit down the pecking order in the group vocally. It was frustrating but I had to admit it was a challenge to deliver vocal harmony parts and play a bass part that wasn't in sync with the vocal parts.

Many of the recordings were played by a session group. I learnt my bass parts primarily from Alan Tarney, who was part of David Mackay's in-house session band. Alan eventually went on to write the song 'We Don't Talk Anymore' which became a huge UK number one hit for Cliff Richard.

25th February – The Mixtures perform 'The Pushbike Song' on *Top Of The Pops*

Amazingly the single has remained at number 2 in the UK charts behind George Harrison's 'My Sweet Lord' for a month.

MICK FLINN: After I had been gigging with The Mixtures near the beach in Melbourne, Australia, I received a phone call from The New Seekers' manager David Joseph, who I knew from his time as a TV producer on the popular music show *Kommotion*.

With David Mackay making him aware of 'The Pushbike Song', which at the time of his call was a big number one hit in Australia, he explained that Polydor wanted to release it as they felt it was going to be a big hit in the UK. He told me that Polydor wanted us to go on *Top Of The Tops*, a programme I had never heard of, to promote the song. I made it clear to David Joseph it was impossible to drop everything and commit immediately as we had concerts in Melbourne.

Asking us how soon we could get over to the UK, I suggested three weeks. The other guys in the band were shocked that we were off to England!

March 1971 - Produced by John Farrar and Bruce Welch, the Olivia Newton John single 'If Not For You' is released on Interfusion

As well as being her first international release it is also her first hit, as it becomes a top 10 hit in the UK and Australia and a top 30 hit in the US. Having played a minor role in The New Seekers story, you could say this is the point where the career of Olivia Newton John begins.

3rd April – Monaco win the Eurovision Song Contest held in Dublin

'Jack in the Box' sung by Clodagh Rodgers comes fourth for the UK, also reaching number four in the UK charts.

26th April – The New Seekers appear on *The Andy Williams Show*

Guests of the popular American singer also include Tommy Roe, most famous for his 1969 international hit 'Dizzy' (later revived as a UK number one hit by Vic Reeves in 1991), and Bobbie Gentry, most famous for hit song 'Ode To Billie Joe'.

May – The New Seekers' third studio album *Beautiful People* is released on Phillips in the UK and by Elektra in the US

There are eleven interpretations whilst the other track is a superb country rock song 'Cincinatti' written by Peter Doyle.

With his working model of giving each member of The New Seekers their individual part to learn before they all come together to record songs in the studio, this is the first album David Mackay entirely produces. He is also, with Bill Shepherd, the arranger on this album.

A FAN'S PERSPECTIVE ON THE ALBUM: With a front cover showing the group smiling and having fun on a roundabout in a kids'

88

playground, this is one of the classic albums by The New Seekers and there are a lot of very good songs on this release.

'When There's No Love Left' demonstrates Eve's vocals but once again it's a song that does have a religious feel to it. Lyn comes to the fore with the song 'I'll Be Home', which always went down well live, and there's a brilliant interpretation of The Move hit 'Blackberry Way'.

PAUL LAYTON: David Mackay and David Joseph basically put their heads together to ensure commercial success was maximised by sourcing the best songs they could find for us. The opportunity for us to have our own material on an album or B side was a bonus. David Mackay had a talent for creating different vocal arrangements on songs that had already been hits for solo artists rather than groups.

KEITH POTGER: By this stage, as with Abba following on from The New Seekers, David Mackay had assembled a really good musical collective based around the group Quartet that came over to the UK from Australia.

For instance the incredible guitar solo on the song 'Never Ending Song Of Love' comes from Terry Brittan, who was actually born in England but went over to Australia writing songs for the group called The Twilights.

As well as co-writing hits for Cliff Richard such as 'Devil Woman', Terry is most famous for writing two classics with Graham Lyle for Tina Turner, 'What's Love Got To Do With It' and 'We Don't Need Another Hero'.

10th to 16th May – The New Seekers top the bill at The Sunderland Empire
Perhaps somewhat perversely, the previous year's Eurovision song contest winner Dana is now one of the supporting acts.

29th May – The New Seekers play The Royal Festival Hall in the UK
Here they support US singer-songwriter Neil Diamond, who is just coming off the back of three enormous hits 'Sweet Caroline', 'Cracklin' Rosie' and 'I Am I Said'.

30th May – The New Seekers again appear on *The Ed Sullivan Show* in the US

Hosted by the singer Jack Jones, they perform their first three singles released in the US.

The other guests were Loretta Lynn (who sang 'I Wanna Be Free', 'Coal Miner', 'Daughter' and a duet with Jack Jones, 'Move It On Home') and a group called Your Father's Moustache (who sang 'Mountain Dew' and '5-Feet-Two').

1st June – The TV movie *Vincent Price Is In The Country* is released

As well as The New Seekers, the cast includes jazz singer Cleo Laine, broadcaster Ned Sherrin and actress Lynn Redgrave, who played the lead in the popular 60s film Georgy Girl, *with the title track of course becoming a big hit song for The Seekers.*

PAUL LAYTON: It was a thrill for the group to take part in a film with that opportunity presented to us by our management.

One of the most memorable parts for me was the time we had to drive separate cars across this field outside the gates of a mansion house in order to meet up with Vincent Price. It was all very precisely set up. Marty had to say the line 'Hey Vincent, I think the house is round the next bend' so that Vincent could respond with something like 'I think I'm going round the bend more like' but of course what happened is that Marty forgot the word 'bend' and said 'corner' instead so the whole thing had to be re-shot!

5th June – 'Chirpy, Chirpy, Cheap, Cheap' by Middle of the Road enters the UK top 40

A hugely catchy song, it eventually tops the UK singles charts. It is focused around Sally Carr's powerful and distinctive vocals.

NIC CULVERWELL: Whilst I'm sure the other members of the group contributed to the sound of that release when you think of Middle Of The Road you think of Sally Carr's singing. On the other hand, when you think of The New Seekers, you don't just think about one vocalist.

The New Seekers were a complete group consisting of five very talented vocalists, although certainly with those early releases there's no denying Eve's voice was the most recognisable.

15th June – The New Seekers appear on BBC1's *Top Of The Pops* hosted by Radio 1 DJ Tony Blackburn performing 'Never Ending Song Of Love'

Released five days earlier, it is a tremendously catchy pop interpretation of a Delaney & Bonnie song and is the last single released by the group on the Phillips label.

Since 'What Have They Done To My Song Ma', two singles had been released. With that third New Seekers single release, 'When There's No Love Left' was on the A side whilst the Melanie Safka song 'Beautiful People' was on the B side, and apparently radio stations chose to play the flip side as it highlighted Eve's lead vocal. After this, 'The Nickel Song', another song by Melanie Safka, was the group's fourth release. Neither releases charted.

DAVID MACKAY: I was invited to go on a ski-ing holiday in Zermatt with Keith Potger and David Joseph during the 1970 Xmas period. As I wasn't a good skier I took on the role of looking after the children instead, so I could continue to work on the arrangements of songs.

KEITH POTGER: We were told beforehand that the rental equipment available at the resort was not very good so consequently we rented skis in England and brought them over. Unfortunately David Mackay's skis were too big for him!

Apart from David Joseph, who I believed had skied a bit, we were all novices. Having spent around three minutes going completely out of control on these gigantic skis, poor David understandably decided to down tools, putting them away for the rest of the holiday. With the equipment we had he was the only sensible one!

DAVID MACKAY: It was during the ski-ing trip to Zermatt where I came up with the yodelling section as an alternative to an instrumental break for 'Never Ending Song Of Love'.

PAUL LAYTON: With 'Never Ending Song Of Love' David had broken down the song so that we were given our harmony and individual vocal parts. We were each given a cassette which contained a recording of our particular section so we'd learn our parts separately. As long as you conscientiously learnt your parts it was amazing how well it all came together.

KEITH POTGER: There's the expression 'you don't have a dog and bark yourself' and by this stage as far as the vocal parts for the group went, although I was still co-manager of the group I left that sort of thing to David Mackay. As far as I was concerned he had such a great handle on the group by then he was the expert, not me.

Eve hit the mark with her vocals so precisely on that song and that yodelling section came off brilliantly.

NIC CULVERWELL: The New Seekers first came onto my radar when I heard 'Never Ending Song Of Love' on the radio and then afterwards saw them perform the song on *Top Of The Pops*.

At the time it was released it was very unusual as it was a pop song with tinges of country in there. You didn't ever hear songs like that in those days.

The images of the group performing that release on TV still resonate with me today.

MARTY KRISTIAN: One moment we were performing on various TV shows and venues to a placid sit down audience, the next we were in front of audiences shouting and screaming, reminiscent of what had been going on with me there in Australia. It was a lot of fun.

NIC CULVERWELL: Watching the group on *Top Of The Pops* perform I was immediately struck by their vocal talent and professionalism. They looked magical to me. Reflecting on their power the only group I can compare them with are US group The Mamas & Papas (whilst they had two female singers, they only had two male singers).

Seeing them perform on *Top of the Pops* was the point where I became hooked. My life started to change dramatically. Being a fan of the group took my focus off everything else going on in my life. Previously a good student, my attention was completely drawn away from school and learning.

Once I became a fan of the group there was no turning back for me!

19th June – The New Seekers guest on ITV's *Val Doonican Show* performing 'Never Ending Song Of Love'
Irishman Val Doonican was a popular singer, who had a relaxed crooning style, renowned for performing songs from his rocking chair.

28th June – The first episode of *Follyfoot* is broadcast on ITV
Made by Yorkshire Television for the ITV network, the TV show was very popular in Britain at that time. It is best remembered as being a twist

on Wuthering Heights *for the modern younger generation as posh horse-loving teenager Dora stays with her uncle, a colonel, at his stables and forms a close attachment with working class ne'er-do-well Steve.*

The series has a very striking and evocative song that introduces each episode called 'The Lightning Tree' by vocal group The Settlers, whose career seems to run in parallel with The New Seekers; for instance they were also guests on It's Cliff *back in February. Although they enjoy critical acclaim and are busy live, they experience little success with their releases other than 'The Lightning Tree', which for many of us is known as 'the theme song from* Follyfoot'.

29th July – The New Seekers perform 'Never Ending Song Of Love' on *Top of the Pops*

With yet another edition presented by DJ Jimmy Savile, this is a repeat of the 15 June appearance. It is also the play out track on the 5th August programme and The New Seekers also appear on the 19th August show.

A favoured group of the British Broadcasting Company, clearly the exposure on the most popular music TV show in the UK would have helped make the song a commercial success.

7th August – 'Never Ending Song Of Love' reaches a peak UK chart position of number 2

Somewhat incredibly it stays at that number two spot for five consecutive weeks. It is first of all kept off the summit by 'Get It On', arguably the best ever song by T. Rex, the coolest group of the moment, then 'I'm Still Waiting' by Diana Ross, a favourite of mainstream BBC Radio One DJ Tony Blackburn, plugging the song to the point the record company release it as a single. With this song The New Seekers are up against quite possibly this female icon's best ever solo release. Bad luck guys but better luck next time!

PAUL LAYTON: We were ecstatic with the success 'Never Ending Song of Love' achieved in the UK!

14th August – The New Seekers appear on the BBC1 TV programme *It's Lulu*

As with Cliff Richard, Cilla Black and Val Doonican, Lulu was a singer, very popular at that time with audiences in the UK, who fronted a show where other performers were guest singers.

However, 'Boom Bang A Bang', the UK entrant for the 1969 Eurovision Song contest, was Lulu's last commercial success, becoming the joint winner of the contest alongside two other songs.

Lulu's next notable single success came in 1974, when her highly regarded interpretation of Bowie song 'The Man Who Sold the World' reached number three in the UK charts.

24th August – The New Seekers appear on Granada TV's *Lift Off with Ayshea*

Other guests included The Move, who performed 'Tonight', a Roy Wood song that garnered a hit for the group even though he apparently wrote it exclusively for The New Seekers, New World who performed what became their hit single, 'Tom Tom Turnaround' and resident dancers The Feet.

September – The album *New Colours* is the group's first release on new label Polydor

MICK FLINN: From my experience Polydor was a good record company to work with. I certainly felt they did as much as they could for our group Springfield Revival.

The hazy cover photograph shows the smiling group posing to the camera in a forest, dressed casually, with Peter Doyle wearing a Mickey Mouse t-shirt. Altogether there are 12 tracks on the album, which include an original from Paul Layton and three tracks from Peter Doyle. The remaining songs are covers, including the group's interpretation of the Roy Wood song 'Tonight'.

In spite of the huge success of single 'Never Ending Song Of Love' the album is The New Seekers' first charting album in the UK, reaching the top 40. The album is later repackaged in the US and retitled We'd Like To Teach The World To Sing, *with the cover shot of the group holding hands while on a mountainside referencing the lyric of that song.*

The album is once again produced and arranged by David Mackay.

94

A FAN'S PERSPECTIVE ON THE ALBUM: With 'Never Ending Song Of Love' being the group's first sizeable UK hit, it is likely this would have been most people's first album experience of The New Seekers.

The feel of New Colours captures the essence of what the group were at that time. It's a perfect selection of songs, with the group performing those songs extremely well. There are so many different songs on the album it would have been difficult to have selected a single to release. 'Doggone My Soul' or 'Good Old Fashioned Music' were the two best possibilities. 'Child of Mine', a beautiful song, has a lyric which references the album title, New Colours. *The three songs by Peter Doyle, 'Move Me Lord', a sombre ballad, 'Boomtown', a rocker, and 'Lay Me Down', with Lyn's subdued vocal, are all quite different in feel, demonstrating his qualities as a very proficient songwriter.*

It's an album that captures the music made by The New Seekers at that time really well.

PAUL LAYTON: In my opinion people weren't aware of our albums until they became fans of the singles.

'Sweet Louise' was a song I wrote about the girl I dated in New York, with the lyrics outlining the discussions we might have had about religion.

I was blown away that Peter sang it and asked me afterwards whether what he did with the vocal was alright or not.

The New Seekers record 'I'd Like To Teach The World To Sing (In Perfect Harmony)', based on one of a series of radio jingles they had already recorded

The New Seekers radio jingle recording forms the basis of a tremendously popular 'just under a minute' TV 'hilltop advert'. First of all there's a close up on the face of a blond actress miming Eve's lead vocal. From there the camera scans skilfully across a hillside of young people from different cultures who are each holding the iconic Coke bottle, with just enough personality and movement to indicate they are not part of a cult, as they sing the song (as best they can, considering they are not The New Seekers) in perfect harmony, suggesting 'Coke as the real thing and what the world wants today' (at the dawn of the 70s). Even on this truncated recording Peter Doyle's 'and keep it company' is the stand out line. The advert is still powerful today, if a little naive and of its time.

DAVID MACKAY: I was approached by songwriters Roger Greenaway and Roger Cook, who had written a commercial for Coca Cola.

They wanted me to arrange a jingle, which had to be a minute long, in the style of 'Look What They've Done To My Song Ma' with that New Seekers sound. I was given a demo cassette of the song, which they wanted me to extend. We recorded that commercial, I believe, around four months before that advert was aired.

KEITH POTGER: We knew Roger Cook as he had brought the song 'Melting Pot' to us, just before he formed the group Blue Mink, with it of course then becoming a hit for them. Roger Cook and Roger Greenway were already successful hit-making songwriters; for instance they wrote 'You've Got Your Troubles' for The Fortunes. They had a song called 'True Love and Apple Pie' and in my opinion those two guys from McCann Erikson managed to get themselves onto a four way songwriting credit for the song. By that time The New Seekers had started to make waves in America because of the hit single they had achieved.

Seemingly no-one within The New Seekers seemed to regard the 'I'd Like To Buy The World A Coke' radio jingle as being particularly amazing. Of course the part sung by the even tempered Peter Doyle 'and peace throughout the land' cut through the song, with for many that being the stand out section.

MARTY KRISTIAN: My memory is that we recorded a series of different radio jingles with Coke executives gauging from audience reaction which of those had the most resonance. I am surprised how things went as at the time I thought it was just a simple song.

EVE GRAHAM: We went into a studio and from memory sang twelve jingles. I don't remember the one they chose for the Coke advert standing out any more than any of the others. There were so many different lengths for each of the commercials. My memory is just that we did a day's work on them all. Whilst recording our album in the US with David Mackay, our manager David Joseph told us on the phone that The Hillside Singers' single release based on the advert was climbing the charts so he wondered whether or not we should record a single based on what we'd done with the advert.

At this 'I'd Like To Buy The World A Coke' recording session other jingles are made, which include 'Sell A Million', forming the basis of a follow up TV advert shown in the US which is longer (at 69 seconds), more subtle but less powerful than the original. It focuses this time on young people from different cultures holding the iconic bottle in different contexts,

96

such as relaxing in a park or taking a break from playing cricket (the cricket bat shown being no doubt weird to that US audience of the time). With the lead vocal by Lyn Paul, it will form the basis of a solo song released later on during the decade. The suggestion is still that Coca Cola is 'the real thing'.

3rd September – The New Seekers perform on BBC1's *We Want To Sing*
The show is presented by popular bearded TV presenter Rick Jones, who hosted Fingerbobs, *a fondly remembered finger puppet British TV show of the time for young children.*

NIC CULVERWELL: At that time there was no way of avoiding The New Seekers.

'Never Ending Song Of Love' sounded wonderful and the radio seemed to gravitate towards that song very easily. I remember that Radio Luxembourg was very supportive of The New Seekers for instance. As I grew up in the radio age in fact it's still unfathomable to me not to have the radio on throughout the day.

On top of this the group seemed to appear on every variety show possible. BBC and ITV were demonstrably happy to have The New Seekers performing on their programmes.

20th September – The New Seekers play Las Vegas
The group played at The Sahara Hotel, a place where Elvis celebrated his 27th birthday in 1962.

97

A shot of the group from the 21st September as they arrive back in the UK.

26th September – The New Seekers tour the UK

Having undertaken three concerts in North America earlier in the month, the group start the tour at The Floral Hall in Southport with it ending at The Queen Elizabeth Hall, London, on October the 16th.

2nd October – The first ever edition of the Saturday night family TV show *The Generation Game* is broadcast on BBC1

Hosted by popular UK presenter Bruce Forsyth, who comes up with a series of catchphrases, this becomes something of a British televisual institution early on Saturday evenings as families compete against families, undertaking tasks and sketches with eventually an individual winner 'against the clock' having to memorise prizes as they pass along a conveyor belt if they are to win those prizes.

'Life is the name of the game and I wanna play the game with you' goes the theme tune...

18th to 30th October – The New Seekers take up a two week residency at The St Regis Hotel Maisonette in New York

PAUL LAYTON: Marty and I made efforts to always visit the places we went to. At that time Lyn and Peter were in a relationship so they were doing their own thing whilst Eve kept to herself.

21st October – The New Seekers perform their new single, 'Good Old Fashioned Music', on *Top of The Pops*. It is the only track released as a single in the UK from their album *New Colours*

Despite also performing it on The Harry Secombe Show *on the 23rd October, it is not a commercial success and does not even reach the UK top 50.*

PAUL LAYTON: It was a great live song and a set opener for many years. A good opening song to a show doesn't necessarily become a hit record.

With hindsight you could say it shouldn't have been released as a single but at the time it was probably the only song we had ready to go out.

EVE GRAHAM: When we were recording we didn't necessarily know the songs that would be put out as singles. From our perspective we just recorded a bunch of tracks and then one would come out as a release.

We were told the song we were going to record, vocal parts were put in front of us by David Mackay, which we learnt, and we just got on with it.

15th November – The Royal Variety Performance at The London Palladium

With guests that include singers Shirley Bassey and Sacha Distel, The New Seekers perform to an audience which includes the Queen. The show is broadcast on the 21st November by London Weekend Television.

99

NIC CULVERWELL: Although they'd had a hit with 'Never Ending Song Of Love', up to this point they hadn't experienced any other hit singles in the UK, so for The New Seekers to appear on this show was a big achievement.

It would have been tremendously exciting for them to perform three songs at this event.

4th December – The New Seekers are guests on TV show *Cilla*
Cilla Black was a popular Liverpudlian singer and with UK hits in the 60s she was just three years into her TV presenting career.

Her BBC1 show continued on into 1976 as she became perhaps most famous for hosting the popular ITV show Blind Date *in the 80s.*

18th December – 'I'd Like To Teach The World To Sing (In Perfect Harmony)' enters the UK charts at number 32

DAVID MACKAY: Before The New Seekers went on a tour of the US, I suggested to Polydor that the group record a full length version of the song, as I knew the Coca Cola commercial would be pretty big. They didn't feel there was any need for that as they saw it as just being a commercial. However, whilst the group were on tour things just went berserk. It was a brilliant TV advert set on an Italian mountainside with what looked like young adults representing the whole world drinking Coke. They just added more voices to The New Seekers' recording, which created a bigger effect vocally.

As a full length version of the advert by The Hillside Singers had reached the lower reaches of the US charts, I remember getting this panicked phone call in New York from David Joseph telling us all that we had to drop everything and go into the studio straight away to record our own full length version.

I had to fly the multi-track over from the UK, go into a studio and then edit it together so I could make a recording that would last three minutes.

We only had one day off that week, which I remember being a Sunday, so that's when it was recorded. We adapted the lyrics, taking out the 'Coca Colas', put in new voices, added a guitar solo, mixed it and mastered it that same Sunday.

It was sent off to the factory and was in the shops the following Friday.

EVE GRAHAM: In my view it's impossible to say why our version of the song became such a big hit.

If you get something simple that is catchy, hummable and you never get bored of (or if you do you can't stop singing it), I guess that is the recipe for something like 'I'd Like to Teach the World to Sing'.

CHRIS BARRINGTON: It's a song that was tremendously well produced by David Mackay.

NIC CULVERWELL: It's not my favourite song by The New Seekers, although I guess no matter what age you are most people will have some awareness of it.

It was an important milestone in the career of The New Seekers. In my opinion as a fan it's one of the few songs that hasn't particularly aged well and is very much of its time!

MICK FLINN: When I became a New Seeker of course I learnt to perfect the line 'and peace throughout the land' which cuts through and lifts the whole song. Peter Doyle sang that phrase with ease. Peter sang everything with ease.

What a great talent Peter was! If I had half of Peter's voice I'd be a happy man... [pause] - in fact if I had a quarter of his voice I'd be a happy man!

PAUL LAYTON: At the time it was one of those freaky things as there was no history of a TV advert and a pop song combining.

Out of all the jingles we performed, it was not something that set my heart on fire as, like with the other boys, I preferred the rockier alternatives we had to sing. It was catchy and had a great message.

The concept of all the different cultures around the hillside worked and I'm sure the advert played a part in driving the single's success.

NIC CULVERWELL: The harmonies in that song were very complicated and highlighted that distinctive New Seekers sound.

24th December – The New Seekers perform 'I'd Like To Teach The World To Sing (In Perfect Harmony)' on the *It's Cliff Richard* show
Olivia Newton John and The Flirtations also guest on this edition.

25th December – BBC1 broadcasts the programme *Christmas Night with the Stars*
As well as The New Seekers, guests include the singers Lulu and Engelbert Humperdinck, most famous for singing 'Release Me', which has the reputation of being the song that kept The Beatles' 'Penny Lane'/'Strawberry Fields Forever', arguably the best double A side single of all time, off the top of the UK charts.

It is interesting to note with the BBC's prime channel that day interspersed with church services, the Queen's message, Rolf Harris, a Sophia Loren/Gregory Peck mid-sixties film, Richard Baker reading the news headlines, and the first Top of The Pops *retrospective of 1971, introduced by Jimmy Savile. Variety entertainment is placed very firmly on the menu for prime time audiences. Billy Smart's Circus, Cilla Black in an* Aladdin *pantomime, Morecambe & Wise, with Andre Previn as the special guest stooge this year and* The Good Old Days, *where there is a strong emphasis on audience participation as they dress up to celebrate* entertainment 'down at the old bull and bush', are all there for the British watching public to enjoy.

It's hard to imagine today, but there was even a spot for The Black & White Minstrel Show, where performers blacked themselves up as performing minstrels. The show ran until 1978.

27th December – *Top of The Pops: Christmas 1971 Part 2* is broadcast on BBC1

The New Seekers perform a live version of 'Never Ending Song Of Love' on the second Top Of The Pops *Christmas retrospective of the year.*

30th December – The New Seekers perform 'I'd Like To Teach The World To Sing (in Perfect Harmony)' live on *Top Of The Pops*

'My Sweet Lord' by George Harrison is the best selling single of 1971 in the UK. However, 'Never Ending Song Of Love' by The New Seekers is the 7th best selling single, whilst 'The Pushbike Song' by The Mixtures is the 6th best selling song of that year!

With an extremely busy end to the year and their latest single 'I'd Like To Teach The World To Sing (In Perfect Harmony)' receiving a lot of TV promotion, what does 1972 hold for The New Seekers?

Chapter 6
1972: The Year Of T. Rex And The New Seekers

IN THE UK IN 1972...
The coal miners go on strike in the early part of the year * Unemployment exceeds 1 million (the first time it has reached this figure since the 30s) * The Duke of Windsor dies (formerly King Edward XIII until he abdicated the throne) * *Jesus Christ Superstar* **makes its West End debut * An outbreak of 'New Seekermania'!**

NIC CULVERWELL: The New Seekers era ran along similar lines to the lifespan of T. Rex. In fact both groups always seemed to be on the same edition of *Top Of The Pops*!

Whilst T. Rex were the cool group of the day, in Marty Kristian The New Seekers had a pin up to rival Donny Osmond and David Cassidy.

There certainly are parallels. Folk group Tyrannosaurus Rex became pop group T. Rex in 1970 as the more staid folk-style mark one version of The New Seekers morphed into the perfect harmonies and the soft pop of the mark two version that year too. Very different in nature to one another, both groups seemed almost tailor made for TV. In the case of The New Seekers there's a strong argument to suggest that at the outset David Joseph and Keith Potger were looking to put a vocal group together that belonged on TV.

However T. Rex became enormous more or less straightaway in the UK, whilst their last top 30 hit (the 1991 re-release of '20th Century Boy') came in 1976. On the other hand, apart from that sole US hit in 1970, The New Seekers were big from 1971-4, yet even after a split their last top 30 hit in the UK happened in 1978. You might argue T. Rex were hugely successful over a shorter time period (1970-1972). The New Seekers, whilst not as huge commercially, were more successful over a longer period.

In terms of the US, T. Rex only had one significant hit there, in 'Bang A Gong (Get It On)', whilst The New Seekers had three hits there: 'Look What They've Done To My Song Ma', 'I'd Like To teach The World To Sing' and 'Pinball Wizard/See Me Feel Me'.

In a population by now of just over 56 million in the UK, only 1.6 million people own colour TV sets, although this had risen from 100,000 in March 1969. Many people had a contract to rent their coloured TVs with

Radio Rentals, a popular company. The idea of owning a television, because it was so expensive to buy a TV set (as they were termed), was just not something people tended to do.

On the 1ˢᵗ, 8ᵗʰ, 15ᵗʰ, 22ⁿᵈ & 29ᵗʰ January, as well as the 5ᵗʰ February, told by their management they have been given this commitment, between 6.15 to 7pm on the *It's Cliff* BBC1 TV show each week The New Seekers perform a song that the public can vote for as the UK entrant for the 1972 Eurovision Song Contest

The Cliff Richard show, hosted by the most respected UK singer of the day, whose music appeals to all age groups, is on prime time British TV just at the point when the whole family are congregated around their TV set after they have eaten their tea.

The hugely popular John Pertwee era Dr Who *preceded the Cliff Richard show, with at that time the January series focused on another Dalek story, whilst the gritty realism (for 1972) of* Dixon Of Dock Green *followed the show, with Jack Warner as the lead policeman character as that programme was now entering its seventeenth year of existence.*

PAUL LAYTON: The New Seekers were chosen to represent the UK at the 1972 Eurovision Song Contest, being an up and coming group.

105

Things were starting to happen for us so my perception is that was why Billy Cotton Junior, head of BBC light entertainment, asked us to be the UK's representative.

KEITH POTGER: I believe there were a few factors that came into play as to why The New Seekers were chosen as the group that would represent the United Kingdom at the Eurovision Song Contest in 1972.

The group had done some work already for the BBC, they were at the forefront of that middle-of-the-road style of music that fitted Eurovision in those days and were regarded as being a very good television commodity.

I can imagine with all the network of connections that David Joseph would have built up within the industry that also would have played a part in the group being chosen.

6th January – The New Seekers perform 'I'd Like To Teach The World To Sing' on *Top of The Pops*
Two days later it became the group's first UK number one.
This clip is repeated on the 13th, 20th and 27th January editions of the programme as it remains at the summit for 4 weeks during that month.

21st January - The group Milkwood release their first single 'Watching You Go' on Anchor Records
The group consists of 21-year-old Chris Barrington on vocals as well as bass guitar, 24-year-old Sally Graham on vocals and Laurie Heath on acoustic guitar/vocals. Of course all three members were part of the first line up of The New Seekers.

Don Hunter is the producer and songwriter, who is later to work on the Stevie Wonder classic album Songs In The Key Of Life.

The single release is not commercially successful.

SALLY GRAHAM: We obtained a record deal with Anchor, which was a subsidiary of the Warner Brothers label, so for a while we were over the moon.

Touring we had a strange little following in places like Sicily, Amsterdam and The Speakeasy in London. We used to play at The Zoom Club in Frankfurt where a guy used to come in with a snake around his neck.

We were managed by John Brewer [later awarded an Ivor Novello for producing and publishing Gerry Rattery's song 'Baker Street'] and I thought we were great. We should have been more successful but I don't think we were pushy enough and we didn't have the big guns in music behind us.

CHRIS BARRINGTON: Going in a folk direction, we formed the group Milkwood, where we released singles although we didn't experience any success.

SALLY GRAHAM: The three of us stayed with that acoustic format; however, we didn't feel we were heading in a mainstream direction and saw ourselves heading more towards that Cat Stevens direction.

We certainly aimed to be cooler than The New Seekers had been before the three of us departed.

29th January – An Eve Graham interview appears in UK inky music newspaper *Record Mirror*
Within the article Eve gives readers wardrobe hints.
Whilst this newspaper, established in 1954, was perhaps the least highly regarded of the British music inkies, with Melody Maker, *set up in 1926, and the* New Musical Express, *founded in 1952, leading the way, (and* Sounds *just starting in 1970 to rival the* NME*), it does suggest that even the serious UK music press were by now taking notice of this New Seeker phenomenon.*

12th February – The New Seekers perform the six songs that are to be considered by the public as the potential Eurovision entrant to represent the UK at the 1972 Eurovision Song Contest in Edinburgh
The public had to cast their vote on a postcard which had to arrive at a specified postal address no later than February 17th for the vote to be considered.

15th February – The Central Electricity Generating Board announces power cuts across the UK
The body, responsible for the UK's electricity supply, took the steps following electricity shortages caused by the miners' strike.
A regional rota was employed for the power cuts, which took place between 7am and midnight. Blackouts could last for up to nine hours at a time, with everything from shopping to homework being done by candlelight.

19th February – On Cliff Richard's show, 'Beg, Steal or Borrow', with that hook expressing to what lengths someone would go to bring love to another person, is announced as the song the public has voted to become the UK entrant for the 1972 Eurovision Song Contest
The New Seekers perform the song on the show.

DAVID MACKAY: Out of the six songs it was the best one. It had a good feeling and harmonically it worked well for the group. For me it wasn't of the same quality as 'Never Ending Song Of Love' or 'Look What They've Done To My Song Ma', but it was still a very good song.

PAUL LAYTON: I think at the time we all felt it would be the winner and that it was the best song. It worked for the group. There was a nice duet there for Lyn and Peter and of course it was also very catchy.

NIC CULVERWELL: In the Midlands we experienced our power cuts at 6pm on Saturdays and as a consequence I never saw this edition.

24th February to 2nd March – The New Seekers' Eurovision song 'Beg, Steal or Borrow' is promoted on BBC1's *Top Of The Pops*
On the 24th February Top Of The Pops, *with Chicory Tip's 'Son Of My Father' at the top of the UK charts, a clip from* It's Cliff Richard *is shown. The same clip is also played on the following week's edition as well as the 2nd March and 30th March programmes, with the group never actually playing the song on* Top of The Pops.

SALLY GRAHAM: For me, the voice of Peter Doyle on 'Beg, Steal or Borrow' makes that record special.

4th March – 'Beg, Steal or Borrow' enters the UK charts at number 12
The single rises to a peak of number two on the 25th March where it remains for three weeks, each week resting behind Nillson's 'Without You', which becomes the biggest selling single in the UK for that year.
Effectively this means the song rests in the number two position two weeks after the UK's defeat by Luxembourg at The Eurovision Song Contest final, suggesting there is unstoppable New Seeker momentum throughout the land despite the group not achieving that hoped-for victory.
Written by three songwriters, the Australian connection still follows the group around as one of the songwriters is Tony Cole, actually Branko

108

Miler, who goes onto write songs for the 1973 film Take Me High, *which is a Cliff Richard vehicle.*

13ᵗʰ March – 'Beg, Steal or Borrow' appears on the BBC programme *A Song for Europe 1972: Part One*
Introduced by Cliff Richard, this programme is the BBC's response to the new ruling that all songs featured in the Eurovision Song Contest must be played in each country ahead of the contest. This programme features the contesting songs from Germany, France, Ireland, Spain, UK, Norway, Portugal, Switzerland and Malta

NIC CULVERWELL: Back in those days Eurovision was a huge occasion that everybody watched and looked forward to. It was a programme that was celebrated rather than being something you were ashamed of watching. It was very much family viewing!

20th March - BBC shows *A Song for Europe 1972: Part Two*
On this programme the remaining songs from Finland, Austria, Italy, Yugoslavia, Sweden, Monaco, Belgium, Luxembourg and the Netherlands are featured.

25th March – Between 9.30pm and 11.10pm, the 1972 Eurovision Song Contest is held at The Usher Hall in Edinburgh

The event should have been held in Monaco, where the previous year's winners came from; however, it is held in Edinburgh as Monaco claim they don't have the facilities to host such a large event.

MARTY KRISTIAN: Before we performed the song in Edinburgh, as it had already reached number two in the UK charts, we were regarded by the press as being hot favourites.

PAUL LAYTON: We actually arrived by train and were whisked off by Rolls Royce from Waverley Station to stay at The Caledonian Hotel in Princes Street. Ironically at the airport there was a banner 'Edinburgh Greets The New Seekers'.

DAVID MACKAY: With the popularity of the group it was manic in Edinburgh. For their own safety the police told the group not to go near the windows. The crowd actually broke down the front door of the hotel they   were   staying   in.

PAUL LAYTON: I remember that the revolving door of the hotel got broken by the fans.
We were told if we went too near the windows we would be arrested for inciting a riot.

DAVID MACKAY: We had police escorts and couldn't really go anywhere or do anything.

PAUL LAYTON: The siege from the fans around the hotel was incredible. In a fit of joyful euphoria I remember Peter Doyle waving his underpants out the window.

DAVID MACKAY: Before the TV recording, Billy Cotton Junior came into the group's dressing room wishing them the best of luck but hoping they'd come second. Basically the BBC only took on the contest that year as Monaco pulled out (it was traditional that the country of the winning song would host the contest the following year) and he was not comfortable for the BBC to host the event twice in a row!

Already number two in the UK charts, surely they are a shoo-in to win? Surely...

NIC CULVERWELL: Fortunately we didn't have a power cut that night. I was very nervous when the group came on stage, watching the group perform with my hands in front of my eyes.

Perhaps reflecting the times, all of the group have shoulder length hair styles (just in the case of Paul Layton). The New Seekers perform their song 5th in the 18 song Eurovision line up.

From left to right on stage, Paul Layton is suitably grooving along, wearing a very dashing spangly suit, almost country in style, plucking his bass next to Lyn, who is in a neck to floor (of its time) pink dress, Peter, hunched over with his acoustic, is in total command as he is tonight the captain of this ship, wearing a light blue suit similar to Paul's, Eve is grooving along very nicely wearing her neck to floor blue dress, slightly more flowing than Lyn's, whilst at that particular time on the far right Marty, the group's pin up, in a black spangly suit, ever the team player is keeping his end up with some great harmonies.

Whilst it's difficult to take your eyes off 'Capt Peter' I have to say right from the first note Lyn is absolutely nailing her vocal and performing wonderfully well. Lyn for me is the star of the show, visibly having fun as she seems completely in her element. Overall it is a very good, confident performance. Well done Britain's The New Seekers.

NIC CULVERWELL: Although I was nervous I remember loving the performance. It was faultless.

In terms of the order of performances, as far as the end voting goes, the British public seemingly have to wait another six songs after 'Beg, Steal or Borrow' before there is another country that presents a challenge to them as Austrian group Milestone, with the 11th song on the night, gain 100 points, coming 5th, with the 1st German entry a strong song coming 3rd and the last Dutch song coming in 4th.

The penultimate song performed is 'Apres Toi', sung by the 22-year-old Greek-born singer Vicky Leandros, in a black dress that messages 'I mean business'. The song starts off slowly, pointing towards ballad territory - in fact it sounds as through nerves perhaps she is singing slightly off key - but then that all changes at 45 seconds into the song as it reaches the chorus, which in English becomes translated as 'Come What May In A World Full Of Changes Nothing Changes My Love For You'. Using hand gestures to sell the song and becoming absorbed by the intensity of her own performance, like Lyn Paul before her, Vicky Leandros is really enjoying herself. Damn her. As well as the hand gestures she's smiling. It's a joyous and skilled performance. Oh dear.

111

NIC CULVERWELL: I remember marvelling at the magnificence of Vicky Leandros and thinking she had put in a really good performance of a great song.

After all 18 songs have been performed, there is a short intermission, as viewers watch kilted bagpipers marching around Edinburgh Castle, and then after that there is the very august atmosphere of the voting for viewers to watch.

The voting is very long winded and watching the process from a 21st century perspective, it's a little confusing. In essence each round consists of three countries casting their audience votes for each song with the highest possible mark being 10 points and the lowest possible mark being 2 points. The rules are such that countries are not allowed to cast votes for their own entrant.

The members of the group recall events differently from reality, as at absolutely no stage in the voting were The New Seekers leaders. There is a shot of the group laughing nervously as at one point they do take the lead but that is only because the vote for Luxembourg has yet to be cast. You could say for a brief moment the UK are constantly leading each round but that is only because they are the fifth country to receive their votes whereas Luxembourg are the seventeenth country out of eighteen to receive theirs.

The sad fact is Luxembourg start and end the voting as winners, trouncing (there is no other word) all before them.

NIC CULVERWELL: Even with being a New Seekers fan I have always felt Vicky Leandros deserved to win. Compared to the UK entry it was the stronger of the two songs. The best song won the contest. I can actually imagine Eve performing this song well. It would really suit her.

Nevertheless. 'Beg, Steal or Borrow' is a great song which sounds fabulous all these years on.

Spain and Malta awarded the UK two points, with only Norway giving the country a maximum score. Interestingly Spain also gave Luxembourg two points whilst the United Kingdom (yes really), a country renowned for fair play, and Yugoslavia gave Luxembourg maximum points.

As much as it might be remembered differently, in short Luxembourg won pretty easily (by fourteen points in fact) and the UK was really at no point in the race for first place.

PAUL LAYTON: It was a disappointment we didn't win as, like with Bucks Fizz, I think it would have opened more doors for us.

Mind you, I believe there was some tactical voting there from Spain and Malta over the Gibraltar crisis [hmm, there's nothing like that British competitive spirit, Paul].

A version of 'Apres Toi' translated into English as 'Come What May' became a huge number 2 hit in the UK.
Ironically, in 1981 David Mackay, in The New Seekers corner for the 1972 contest, produced practically all of the songs on the Vicky Leandros album Love Is Alive. *All is fair in love, war and song!*

27th March – Two days after that Eurovision final, for the first time live fans contribute to New Seekermania as the group begin their UK tour at The Kelvin Hall in Glasgow

The group play 24 consecutive dates, the last one being at the ABC in Northampton on the 22nd April.

PAUL LAYTON: We hadn't realised the impact of the exposure we had been receiving by appearing on the Cliff Richard show and in representing the UK at Eurovision. You might say there was a Beatlemania/Bay City Rollers reaction to us.

To start with we didn't have any security in place so that had to be sorted out pretty quickly.

I remember we were playing Newcastle on the second date of the tour and the audience of largely girls rushed the stage. The males in the group took off out the back leaving the girls to nearly get mown down.

After that there were security firms with the big guys at the front of the stage.

We were tremendously well received on that tour.

KEITH POTGER: By this stage my role had changed, as I was concentrating on the music publishing side of things as opposed to musical production, which suited me fine.

I was focusing on co-writing songs with British songwriters, which took me away from having a day to day managerial role with the group.

30th March – The New Seekers play The Birmingham Odeon

NIC CULVERWELL: My mother tried to ring the venue but was unable to get through. I was mortified.

By then my focus on education had gone. There were no qualms about it: skipping afternoon lessons, I got on a bus to Wolverhampton where I caught a train to Birmingham New Street. Going to the venue, as I was only buying a ticket for myself, I was lucky enough to get a seat one row from the front next to the aisle.

On the night of the show I was sitting right in front of Lyn Paul and Peter Doyle. I remember I grabbed the person's arm next to me because I was so shocked to see my favourite group in the flesh, having only previously seen them on TV. They really existed as human beings!

I remember the group played two sets with an interval in between. They ended their first set with 'Teach The World To Sing'.

There was a certain degree of hysteria, although the audience didn't just include teenagers and people were seated. The management of the group knew their audience and with a variety of age groups following the group they brought in ballads such as 'Come Softly To Me'.

From my understanding, the atmosphere became rowdier as the tour progressed.

24th April – The New Seekers play The Royal Albert Hall
This performance is recorded. As well as being broadcast by BBC1 on the 23rd July it is released as a live album in November, which does not chart.

NIC CULVERWELL: At the time, with the release coming just before Christmas, it was something you couldn't wait to get your hands on.

Technically it is well produced and the sound is full. Now I believe it is an album of its time. There are some great songs on the album such as 'When There's No Love Left', 'Angel Of The Morning' with Eve on lead vocals and the Nillson song 'One' with Peter Doyle on lead vocals. Some songs don't fit well on the album, for instance 'When I Was Small' with Lyn and Peter reminiscing about the times they were children, but that's because the song is very visual, which is the same with Lyn performing 'I'm A Nut', which is effectively a dance routine.

When I compiled The New Seekers box set this was the album everybody wanted to see on CD. New Seekers albums had previously tended to be overlooked as releases in the CD format.

For the 21st century listener it is not an easy listen and to me it doesn't represent The New Seekers as they should be heard.

114

8th April – The New Seekers album *We'd Like To Teach The World To Sing*, with the group relaxed on the front cover in front of Edinburgh Castle (an obvious Eurovision reference), reaches a UK peak of number 2 in the charts

The album released with the same title in the US at the back end of 1971 is essentially a repackaging of the New Colours *album release but, as any Eurovision reference would be lost on the US audience, the cover shows the group holding hands 'in perfect harmony' on a mountainside. As with the UK release, it achieves the group's highest ever placing there too, reaching number 37 in the Billboard charts.*

The twelve tracks on the album, which is produced and arranged by David Mackay, include a Marty Kristian and Peter Doyle song. As well as this, the two huge 1972 hits are on the album, with the other tracks group interpretations as Eve, Lyn, Peter and Marty all have at least one lead vocal.

A FAN'S PERSPECTIVE ON THE ALBUM: This album was released to coincide with Eurovision, as is messaged by the cover art shot. It represented the group at their most commercial with 'Teach The World To Sing' and 'Beg, Steal or Borrow' on there and it was their biggest ever commercial success, reaching number 2 in the UK charts. It features the song 'One by One' which many people feel should have been the song that went forward as the UK entrant for Eurovision alongside all the other songs that made the UK final. 'Songs of Praise' written by Roy Wood of The Move and later Wizard was a strange song. The album also contained 'The World I Wish For You' which was one of the Coca Cola jingles. Cilla Black released this as a single during the course of the year, charting outside the UK top 50. Unlike 'Just An Old Fashioned Love Song' the group's interpretation of 'Changes IV' does fit The New Seekers style.

13th April – The first episode of *Love Thy Neighbour* is broadcast on British TV

Produced by Thames Television for the ITV network, the central theme of this comedy series is the verbal sparring between black and white male neighbours. The writers admit each episode included both anti-white and anti-black sentiment, and as such it could be regarded as ITV dealing with 'the race issue' through comedy.

The views of the central white male character were presented to make him appear ignorant and bigoted, contrasted with the more tolerant attitude of his wife. 'In nearly every show, the white neighbour was shown to be wrong', Rudolph Walker, the actor who played the black central male character, wrote in 2001.

The male black character is portrayed as better educated, although also stubborn and consistently uses insulting phrases to describe his white neighbour.

Very popular at the time, it was also criticised in the media of the time. There are 53 episodes across eight series, with the last broadcast airing on the 22ⁿᵈ January 1976.

10ᵗʰ June – The New Seekers single 'Circles' first enters the UK Chart

This fantastic interpretation of a Harry Chapin song eventually achieves a peak position of number 4 in the UK charts

DAVID MACKAY: I really liked the song and tried to make the arrangement seem as though the sound was spinning around with those harmonies.

With a gentle treatment of the song I tried to make it as unique as I could.

EVE GRAHAM: Whenever I sing 'Circles' I always have the same emotion. It still has the same meaning to me having performed the song now for around 50 years.

In being able to sing as soon as the music starts you are right into the sensation and feeling of the song.

Every time I sing 'Circles' I still feel the same emotion and because of that I can express that emotion.

NIC CULVERWELL: I heard the group trialling the song on their UK tour after the Eurovision final and, although it became tremendously popular amongst the fans, the reason why there is no introduction applause on that live recording of The Royal Albert Hall performance is quite simply it was a song that wasn't known then.

Quite understandably 'Circles' is many people's favourite New Seekers song.

15ᵗʰ June – The New Seekers perform 'Circles' on *Top of The Pops*

This performance is repeated on the June 22 and July 6 editions of the show. The 6ᵗʰ July edition, hosted by Tony Blackburn, included that unique Bowie performance of 'Starman' as he points at the camera when he sings the line 'picked on you', though it is more famous for the moment he drapes his arm over lead guitarist Mick Ronson: a male touching a male on TV in those days really was taboo and groundbreaking.

NIC CULVERWELL: This song marked a mature change in direction as, although with 'Beg, Steal or Borrow', Lyn and Peter shared lead vocals, the group reverted back to Eve and Peter sharing lead vocals.

July – Larrie Myers' Gem amalgamates with the Toby Organisation to become the Gem-Toby Organisation, most famously known as GTO

KEITH POTGER: It was a great move at this point in time as for instance Gem had Mike Leander producing Gary Glitter and Tony De Fries involved with David Bowie. As they were heavy hitters it seemed, as Elektra in the US aimed to take The New Seekers under their wing, a good strategic move from which we could expand the reach of the group and grow another branch in The New Seekers' family tree.

14th July – The debut single by Springfield Revival 'You'll Always Be On My Mind' is released on Polydor

A promotional photograph of Springfield Revival showing from left to right Mick Flinn, Donna Jones and Ray Martin. Mick Flinn and Donna Jones are later to join The New Seekers.

MICK FLINN: After The Mixtures' tour of the UK the other guys got homesick and returned to the sun of Australia, whilst I stayed on in the UK, as I felt my future lay here. As a result David Joseph got to hear about this and asked me if I'd be interested in joining the group he was looking to set up, which became Springfield Revival.

DONNA JONES: I had been supporting The New Seekers when their management (David Joseph and Keith Potger) got in touch with my manager in order to arrange a time for them to meet with me. From that meeting Keith phoned me up to tell me that he wanted me to join this new group Springfield Revival as their lead singer. I'm sure Lyn would have put a good word in for me as we were still good friends. I was over the moon!

MICK FLINN: As with The New Seekers, who were a tribute to The Seekers, Springfield Revival was established to take the musical baton from The Springfields and be a tribute to that group.

Initially we were going to perform the songs of The Springfields as well as folk songs.

118

DONNA JONES: I wasn't sure what to think about Mick Flinn the first time I met him, as with his big cowboy hat and bomber jacket he came across as very much the pop star. Sorta of too cool for school, I guess. On the other hand there I was with my white plastic boots and mini skirt straight from Manchester. I didn't feel like I fitted in and to be honest I felt quite uncomfortable [Mick and Donna are now married].

MICK FLINN: I wasn't wearing a bomber jacket; it was a very expensive cowskin jacket!

DONNA JONES: It was so short!

MICK FLINN: Ray was good looking and had a Tommy Steele look. He'd come straight from theatre, having a stage school background, and had been in a musical. Ray had a cool London boy look.

DONNA JONES: We were very much a manufactured group. Ray was just 17 and was thrown in at the deep end. Keith had the daunting task of not only teaching Ray the guitar but also teaching us all the harmonies for the songs. We set to work straight away.

MICK FLINN: Keith had to teach Ray from scratch. Ray Martin had never played the guitar before so he practised until his fingers bled. He'd never worked on harmonies before either!

DONNA JONES: He was a talented guy though. Our manager David Joseph thought he was amazing!

As with The New Seekers, David Joseph and Keith Potger co-manage Springfield Revival.

MICK FLINN: Unlike performers today, when we were given a contract you wouldn't dispute anything as if you did they'd find someone else.

DONNA JONES: We were paid twenty-five pounds a week but with the management company's track record in bringing success to The New Seekers you didn't really question anything.
  I thought they're going to make us stars and they were going to get us regular work. We were very naive, unlike performers today who are so clued in.

119

MICK FLINN: As was the case with The New Seekers, our booking agents were Freya and Slim Miller. I remember meeting them first of all with The Mixtures when we came to the UK for the tour and they explained where they were going to book us. They were really great at their jobs and Freya in particular was a really good businesswoman.

I remember Freya telling Donna to wear these long dresses, which were a bit old fashioned for that time. We were controlled by others but they were great days.

David's aim was for us to become a top-of-the-bill act straight away so we had to rehearse like crazy!

If David Joseph had a vision to do something, he would see it right through. He had a great instinct about what would work which you just had to go along with as he was often right.

After several months in the group Donna and Mick develop a romance together.

MICK FLINN: David Joseph was ruthless. He gave Donna and myself an ultimatum: 'it's either the group or the relationship, not both' when we became an item. In other words, one of us could stay in the group if we continued our relationship, not the two of us, unless of course we broke up.

He'd had that experience already you see with Lyn Paul and Peter Doyle as apparently when they had an argument they'd take it on stage with them.

DONNA JONES: Consequently we pretended that we'd broken up but carried on with our relationship discreetly.

MICK FLINN: We told David Joseph we'd broken up but stayed together!

Keith Potger and John Pantry, who has engineered songs for The New Seekers, have co-written, produced and arranged this single.

MICK FLINN: John Pantry was a lovely guy.

DONNA JONES: We'd go into the church hall in St John's Wood five days a week and Keith had already worked out all the arrangements.

MICK FLINN: We'd work almost 9-5 each day on the songs with everything going in this folk direction.

120

DONNA JONES: At the end of each day he'd give each of us a cassette with all our parts we had to learn for the next day. We'd do this for about six months every single day with Keith being there as well.

Effectively the group become the stablemates of The New Seekers, as is shown in this release, as it is very much a joint effort between John Pantry, who has been the engineer for The New Seekers, and Keith Potger, who of course is still The New Seekers' co-manager with David Joseph.

MICK FLINN: We were top of the bill in cabaret venues whilst The New Seekers were headlining big venues when we were a support act at those concerts.

Whilst we were in the UK, The New Seekers were in the US, and vice-versa. We were in the same stable, being on that Gem-Toby roster, but we weren't running along the same paddock. In fact I can't ever remember Springfield Revival playing on the same bill as The New Seekers.

I knew Peter and Marty already from Australia. My first group, The Wild Colonials, had already backed Marty on the recording in Ossie Byrne's studio for his first TV show. I met Paul through Ossie Byrne, who was producing him at the time.

The single is not a commercial success.

DONNA JONES: With the opportunities we were given, I can't understand why we never had hit singles. We performed on all the big TV shows of the day and we were a support on major world tours, for instance The Osmonds in 1973.

MICK FLINN: It was very difficult. When you think about it, in those days thousands of songs were released each day with very few of them becoming hits.

The songs we wrote were never chosen as releases. Having hit singles is always a question of having the right songs. You need the right songs at the right time. We just didn't have those songs!

That year their first self-titled album was also released. With The New Seekers being produced by David Mackay, it is interesting to note this album is produced by Keith Potger, who also arranges three songs and co-writes another.

MICK FLINN: I think they were trying to push us in a folk direction. In a sense he was getting others to do what he really wanted to do himself.

121

Keith was a great catalyst to get us going. We never much liked that folk direction we felt we had to go in.

David Joseph and Keith Potger had been successful with The New Seekers so we felt they could make us successful too. We tried to change the formula by including some country and pop songs in our set, which always went down well. In the end we kinda went against the grain with what we were supposed to do.

DONNA JONES: The problem with that first album for me was we didn't have a clear musical direction.

MICK FLINN: To be fair, at that time Keith Potger did encourage Donna and myself to write songs.

In 1973 Springfield Revival release a second album on Polydor called Highlights. *Once again it is co-produced by John Pantry and Keith Potger but once again it is commercially unsuccessful.*

MICK FLINN: I felt that the songs were better on this album. Our stage act was very folk orientated to start with but by the time of *Highlights* we put a bit of our own personality on there. It was a bit more pop and heading towards that New Seekers territory.

There is also another self-titled third album released in 1973 in the US, with most tracks produced by that Potger/Pantry combination, although two tracks are produced by Michael Lloyd and arranged by Tommy Oliver. Released this time on MGM, it once again fails to chart.

15ᵗʰ July to the 12ᵗʰ August – The New Seekers perform on Ken Barry's *Wow* show in the US
This was a free form comedy variety show with musicians also performing on it.
The New Seekers sang 'I'd Like To Teach The World To Sing (In Perfect Harmony)' on the 15ᵗʰ July show when Cass Elliot of The Mamas & The Papas was a guest, whilst famous comedian George Burns was with them on the 22ⁿᵈ July show when they performed 'Circles'. The Saturday Night Live *personality Steve Martin appears with Terri Garr, most famous for starring in* Tootsie *and* Close Encounters Of The Third Kind, *and the group on the 29ᵗʰ July edition, as well as them both being with The New Seekers on the 12ᵗʰ August show.*

26th August - The album *Never Ending Song Of Love* reaches a peak position of 35 in the UK charts

Arguably you could say this is a repackaging of the Beautiful People *album release that aims to ride off the back of the group's run of commercial success; however, there is no group shot on the roundabout, the title of course is different, the running order with the tracks has changed and there is no 'There's A Light' as instead the fan has 'Alright My Love'.*

In a sense there is a second chance to hear the material from Beautiful People *now that the group has a wider audience. However, the repackaging and release is somewhat strange with a new album literally round the corner.*

September – The album *Circles* is released

Once again this is an album produced and arranged by David Mackay. There are nine covers, as well as a Marty Kristian/Paul Layton co-write in 'Idaho', 'Reap What You Sow', a great rock song by Marty Kristian, and two songs by Peter Doyle.

The album reached number 23 in the UK but only made a chart position of 166 in the US. The US version, however, was more or less the album released previously in the UK as We'd Like To Teach The World To Sing.

A FAN'S PERSPECTIVE: It is commonly accepted 'I Saw The Light' should have been The New Seekers' next single rather than 'Come Softly To Me'. It is written by Todd Rundgren and is a most fabulous rock song highlighting the vocals of Lyn Paul in a different musical context. Whilst the group perform great interpretations of 'Day By Day', Carole King's 'Beautiful' and Dylan's 'Blowin' In The Wind', their interpretation of 'Morning Has Broken' misses the mark. It also contains the soft rock of 'Reap What You Sow', which many people regard as being one of Marty's best songs for The New Seekers. The circular cover opened up into segments; it was a bit like peeling an orange and was difficult to manage.

MARTY KRISTIAN: I love what David did with his production of my song 'Reap What You Sow'.

With Peter's lead vocal I would have liked the group to go more in that direction. Around the time of *Circles* I have great memories of how well we all got along with each other. In fact we all lived in California for a while.

DAVID MACKAY: Songs were chosen on their merit. Members of the group that wrote songs would send them to me and if I thought they were good enough I'd record them. I was always flying off to somewhere in Australia, the UK and US, meeting with publishers, searching out songs that were right for the group.

MARTY KRISTIAN: I would say at that time Peter Doyle was the most prolific writer. Possibly I felt a bit overshadowed, not wanting to push what I'd written. I didn't tend to play my songs to anyone in those days. However, David Mackay selected the songs for us.

We trusted David Mackay's judgement as he'd been responsible for quite a few hits and was listening to what was out there in those days.

14th October – The Cat Stevens album *Catch Bull At Four* reaches a peak position of number 2 in the UK charts

An artist who successfully traverses the route of being commercially successful at the same time as being highly regarded critically, unlike The

New Seekers, he perhaps reaches a peak with this album, most especially as it is his sole number one release in the US. Unlike The New Seekers, by this stage he was more successful as an album artist as his biggest UK hit single, 'Father and Son' from 1967, was behind him now.

Although like The New Seekers in being acoustic orientated, he had the added pressure of being an artist who wrote and performed his own songs.

KEITH POTGER: At that time acoustic music was moving away from being middle of the road, which was the market we were originally aiming at.

November – The New Seekers album *Live at The Albert Hall* is released

NIC CULVERWELL: The concert was released as a Betamax and VHS video but not all the songs were included on that. Some years later it was issued on DVD.

Unfortunately if it was released today as a DVD in the 21st century it wouldn't sell!

6th November – The New Seekers appear on a BBC2 broadcast that celebrated 50 years of music

Songs from the decades are performed by a wide range of artists including Vera Lynn, musical hall star Henry Hall, Cliff Richard, Lulu and Gilbert O' Sullivan. The New Seekers interpret 'Smile' in formal attire as the males play instruments whilst the girls are wearing peach coloured ball dresses. There's some great harmonising, with Peter Doyle's voice in particular shining through.

As well as this there is also a medley. Excerpts sung include parts from the songs 'Bye Bye Love', 'Catch A Falling Star', 'Magic Moments', featuring a Marty Kristian lead vocal, and 'Scarlet Ribbons', with a Lyn Paul lead vocal.

Peter Doyle is clearly the least comfortable performer as he sits, somewhat static, on a bar stool. The broadcast is repeated on December 27th.

17th November – The New Seekers appear on *The Sonny & Cher Comedy Hour*

125

With Sonny & Cher most noted for the iconic 60s baroque pop hit 'I Got You Babe', The New Seekers participate in some comedy sketches and perform the single 'Come Softly To Me'.

2nd December – With a Marty lead vocal, The New Seekers single release 'Come Softly To Me' begins its chart run in the UK with the release also demonstrating how well the soft female vocals blend together

This song is produced by Michael Lloyd, as opposed to David Mackay, and arranged by Tommy Oliver, with Marty receiving a 'featuring' credit. It did eventually rise into the top 20 early in 1973.

There is a Top Of The Pops *broadcast for the song on the 14th December and a New Seekers promotional appearance on the 24th December edition of* The Golden Shot, *with young pianist and* Opportunity Knocks *sensation of the time Bobby Crush on the show also.*

PAUL LAYTON: We used to call it 'the dum dum song'. It was very much in keeping with The Fleetwoods' original interpretation with that retro 50s ballad feel.

NIC CULVERWELL: It was a lovely song but to me it has always been a very good B side or album track. It was a strange release considering how successful the previous, more commercial single releases had been that year.

KEITH POTGER: As the group had signed with MGM in the US, Mike Curb, the company's president at the time, hooked the group up with Mike Lloyd and Tommy Oliver.

David Joseph looked towards the American market as being where the future of the group lay. One way of doing this was to use an American producer and arranger. Those connections also led to Springfield Revival, another group on our roster, undertaking a tour with The Osmonds.

There was a definite continental shift away from Europe and the UK towards North America at that time.

EVE GRAHAM: Keith had faded into the background and by then we saw David Joseph as our manager. I didn't know what was going on behind the scenes but all of a sudden David Mackay wasn't there anymore and we were working with someone else in LA.

I never questioned what was going on with the business side. We just had to get on with the job of performing.

126

17ᵗʰ December – A concert for fans of The New Seekers takes place at The Hammersmith Palais in London

The concert is hosted by Ed Stewart, the Radio 1 DJ and presenter of popular Friday evening TV show Crackerjack. *8000 people attend and there is pandemonium as the group are mobbed by hysterical fans.*

NIC CULVERWELL: I remember the concert was organised very suddenly and that you could get hold of two tickets only via the group's fan club.

Apparently 3000 fans got turned away and had to watch *Oliver* at the nearby cinema instead, although the group came over to say hello. It took place during the mid afternoon with the doors opening at one o'clock.

I was one of the lucky ones in being able to get a ticket. As soon as you gained entry into Hammersmith Palais you had to run to the front of the stage. It was so exciting, as a young fan, it really, really was.

25th December – Escaping 1972 New Seekermania in the UK, the group fly to the US

They leave on same day as a clip of 'I'd Like To Teach The World To Sing (In Perfect Harmony)' is shown on BBC1's Top of The Pops *retrospective of the year's music.*

KEITH POTGER: To a certain extent Peter Doyle was always something of a 'loose cannon'. He was certainly fairly easily distracted, shall we say.

People within The New Seekers' family who knew him well were solicitous of his well being and in that role they were able to keep him on track. However, I would say from the back end of 1972 to the start of 1973 we all began to realise Peter needed help.

Number 1 'Without You', Harry Nilson's cover of a Badfinger song, is the best selling single in the UK whilst 'I'd Like To Teach The World To Sing (in Perfect Harmony)' is the fourth best selling single, 'Beg Steal Or Borrow' is the 14ᵗʰ best selling single and 'Circles' is the 33ʳᵈ best selling single.

It is the group's most successful year but what will 1973 hold, as the objective seems to be that they become more popular in the US, building on that very early success there?

Chapter 7
1973: A Change Of Momentum And Direction - Seeking Renewed Harmony With A New Singer

IN THE UK IN 73...
Replacing Sean Connery, Roger Moore is the new James Bond in the film Live & Let Die ** The UK joins the European Economic Community (EEC) * IRA bombs at King's Cross and Euston Stations injure 13 people * Pizza Hut opens its first restaurant in the UK * The album* Dark Side Of The Moon *by Pink Floyd is released*

January 18 - Kennedy Centre, Washington DC
Taking things in their stride, nevertheless The New Seekers are honoured to be on the bill for the event celebrating President Nixon's second term in office, the first time an act from outside the USA has been invited to perform at such an occasion.

PAUL LAYTON: When we went to LA for a period of time we were on the MGM label, with musician Mike Curb the chief executive there. As he had taken an anti drug stance with artists on the label, which had been well received by Richard Nixon, he had been given the role of organising the entertainment for the event. I distinctly remember seeing letters from Nixon spread out all over his desk.

All the acts that were due to play were put on a 747. I remember a grand piano being in the middle of the plane which was where I met Micky Dolenz of The Monkees for the first time.

Of course it was an honour to be part of that but obviously the security was tight. For instance, I remember we had passes that changed colour when they were no longer valid.

January 22nd to January 29th – The New Seekers appear on US TV shows
Co-hosted by Anthony Quinn, most memorable musically for his unusual, gravelly rendition of 'Wandrin' Star' which was a huge UK hit in 1970, The New Seekers appear on The Mike Douglas Show *on the 22nd January, whilst on the 26th January they appear on* The Tonight Show

starring Johnny Carson, *hosted that day by Mama Cass, and return to appear on* The Mike Douglas Show *on the 29th January.*

17th February – The New Seekers appear on the *Cilla* TV show
This time it is Cliff Richard himself who will be representing the UK in the 1973 Eurovision Song Contest and on this edition he sings 'Help It Along', although 'Power To All Our Friends' is ultimately chosen by the British public as the song that will represent the UK at that year's Eurovision Song Contest. It is a song produced by David Mackay.

DAVID MACKAY: Sadly, I took over because Cliff's long term producer Norrie Paramour was ill. Peter Gormley, Cliff's manager, called me to say that he would be looking at a number of producers but that he wanted me to be the first one. It was a daunting task taking over from someone who was responsible for so many hits because if you failed it didn't make you look too good.

March – The album *Now* is released in the UK
There are cartoon drawings of the group on the cover whilst it is retitled Pinball Wizards *in the US. It scrapes the top 50 in the UK but is a long way off entering even the top 100 in the US.*

Although David Mackay produces and arranges four tracks, including 'Look, Look' by Marty Kristian, the other tracks are produced by Michael Lloyd and arranged by Tommy Oliver, including their next single, 'Pinball Wizard/See Me Feel Me'. The 12 tracks include a Marty Kristian/Peter Doyle co-write called 'Time Limit' as well as two tracks written by The Osmonds.

A FAN'S PERSPECTIVE ON THE ALBUM: The photograph the cover is based on is fantastic but the adapted version loses a lot of detail and just isn't as good.

The album released in the US was entitled Pinball Wizards *with the group photograph you assume taken around a pinball machine. It is a much better cover and title. The title* Now, *with the group having a potentially huge hit on their hands with 'Pinball Wizard/See Me Feel Me', doesn't market the album well.*

It wasn't the most coherent of albums; for instance, the arrangement of 'Going Back' with that strange chorus of children in there just doesn't work. However, there is some strong material on the album, like for example the Marty song 'Look, Look', and there's a great vocal from him on 'Time Limit'. 'Everything Changing' is a very US sounding song with Lyn's lead vocal. 'Rain' was on there but that had been recorded two years previously so it doesn't really fit in well. The Osmonds song 'That's My Guy' worked for them but doesn't work for The New Seekers. 'Brand New Song' and 'Somebody Somewhere' are good album tracks. Maybe Michael Lloyd and Tommy Oliver were still adjusting to the sound of the group.

10th March – The New Seekers' single release 'Pinball Wizard/See Mr Feel Me' reaches a UK chart high of 16 and also makes the top 30 in the US

The New Seekers promote the single on BBC1's February 15th Top Of The Pops *with a film clip which is also used on the 1st March edition. The song is played on the 2nd March edition of* Crackerjack *with Thin Lizzy on the show performing their first UK hit, 'Whiskey In The Jar'.*

NIC CULVERWELL: At the time there was shock and consternation in the music press that a group like The New Seekers had the audacity to record an interpretation of a rock song by The Who, one of the world's biggest groups. Quite frankly, as a fan this whetted my appetite for the release!

On hearing it for the first time I thought it was a wonderful and refreshing change of direction for the group.

Marty and Peter perform the first two verses, then Peter and Lyn sing the 'See Me Feel Me' section as the whole group join forces at the end of the song with the final choruses.

I think to the fans it wasn't really so much of a change of direction as we'd heard The New Seekers perform songs like this before with 'Boomtown' and similar appearing on albums already.

PAUL LAYTON: We would have probably got David Mackay in as producer but I believe it was difficult with where we were and how busy he was.

Tommy Oliver arranged the track and Michael Lloyd produced it. The thinking behind the medley idea was based around The Fifth Dimension combination of 'Aquarius' and' Let The Sunshine In', two songs from the musical *Hair*.

MICK FLINN: I was a huge Tommy Oliver fan with the arrangement he did for The New Seekers with Mike Lloyd there producing. He was also the arranger for that Osmonds album from 1973, *The Plan*.

Tommy Oliver came on board with arrangements for Springfield Revival's third album. We'd done some great recordings in the UK with orchestras already. Tommy invited us into the studio when we were recording the backing tracks and saw the 40 piece orchestra he used. He was so professional. The sound was just phenomenal.

I was almost pinned to the back wall.

PAUL LAYTON: We really enjoyed rocking out on that track and Peter Doyle produced a great vocal.

It was nice to get a telegram from songwriter Pete Townshend informing us that he really appreciated our version.

MICK FLINN: The way Tommy Oliver arranged those sections of two different songs makes it sound like one great song. It all works.

It was a different direction for The New Seekers to go in but it was a great direction. It was probably the rockiest thing they ever did.

KEITH POTGER: That single release really highlighted the depth of the group's talent, shifting the emphasis away from the females in the group towards the males.

MICK FLINN: The New Seekers' interpretation of 'Pinball Wizard' is probably the most commercial version of that song recorded.

Keith loved folk music but with that second line up I believe The New Seekers went in more of a pop direction, losing that folk influence with the songs they interpreted. On the other hand, I think Springfield Revival represented a chance for Keith to go back into that folk direction which he loved so much.

NIC CULVERWELL: I think there was awareness by the management there had to be a fresh intake of breath to re-establish the group in the US, which may well have been the reason why Tommy Oliver and Michael Lloyd came on board, as they of course made music for the US market.

22nd March – The New Seekers perform once again at London's Royal Albert Hall

NIC CULVERWELL: I'd gone to see them play at that concert and with time to spare beforehand I decided to visit the offices of The New

Seekers Fan Club in St James Street, where I was welcomed by Jill Webster, who asked me if I'd like to help out.

This turned into three days of opening letters and parcels sent to the group.

When The New Seekers came into the office I remember Eve asking me who I was and that I responded by saying 'I'm Nic. Who are you?' To which she walked away from me. Understandably!

Through nerves I became too cool for school.

27th March – The New Seekers' stablemates Springfield Revival perform at The Dorothy Chandler Pavilion in Los Angeles for the 1973 Academy Awards, the year *The Godfather* won best picture
Nominations for this category were introduced by the legendary Ben Hur *leading actor Charlton Heston.*

MICK FLINN: We were supposed to be having a break when we played in LA at the awards ceremony.

DONNA JONES: It was amazing how David Joseph secured us this opportunity.

MICK FLINN: 'Come Follow, Follow Me' was the play out song at the end of the film *The Little Ark* and was nominated for an Oscar in the Original Song for a Picture category. On reading a newspaper David Joseph had spotted this.

Coincidentally this was a song we had recorded previously from Keith Potger hearing it and feeling it would suit Ray's voice.

Discovering they had no artist to perform the song, after he had sent the Academy a recording and a photograph of the group, they welcomed the idea of Springfield Revival performing the song at this prestigious event.

For an unknown group to appear on a show watched by a global TV audience of 100 million viewers was just phenomenal. David Joseph was a very clever man.

Before Springfield Revival perform the song nominated, incidentally the Oscar is won by the song 'The Morning After' from disaster movie The Poseidon Adventure, *and a 14-year-old Michael Jackson performs his hit song 'Ben', from the horror movie of the same name where a lonely boy befriends a rat.*

MICK FLINN: Although we shared a dressing room, I don't remember talking to Michael Jackson other than the two of us saying hello to each other.

He was in and out of the dressing room running through his song. Effectively when he was on the studio floor we were in the dressing room and vice versa.

7th April – The Eurovision Song Contest final takes place in Luxembourg, the country that defeated the UK into 2nd place the previous year

New Seekers producer David Mackay takes on the mantle of producing the Cliff Richard song 'Power To All Our Friends' representing the UK.

This time the UK dropped a place to come third, with Spain the runners up, and Luxembourg win again as French-born Anne-Marie David is singing their entry. The New Seekers' backing band for many recordings, developed from the debris of Quartet, are on the Cliff Richard recording with mainstays Alan Tarney and Terry Britten on there too.

Entitled 'Tu te reconnaîtras '('I recognised you' is the direct English translation), the winning song is released in the UK as 'Wonderful Dream' and only reaches number 13 in the chart whilst the stirring Cliff Richard pop song is a number one in many European countries, reaching a chart position of number four in the UK. You could say that the UK audience for Eurovision, in choosing 'Power To All Our Friends', prefer this pop direction in favour of the intense ballads that have now won out with voters in the other European countries over the last two years. There again, maybe it is just a case of tactical voting...

This 1973 contest holds the record for the most watched Eurovision Song Contest EVER in the United Kingdom, with an estimated 21.54 million tuning in on the night.

Eurovision was clearly at the peak of popularity that year in the UK, with the whole family watching the contest round their TV set. The following year, the year of Abba, with Olivia Newton John representing the UK, audience viewing figures declined. Was this because they felt the rest of Europe was out of step with the UK's pop taste? Perhaps it was because the UK hadn't won for a while, or quite simply was it because it was beginning to develop its 'naff' image? Strange to think that might have begun in 1974, as from my memory it was a very strong competition at the top end of things that year, and of course Abba won with 'Waterloo'.

133

14th April – The New Seekers song 'Nevertheless' reaches a UK peak chart position of 34

Appearing just over a month after 'Pinball Wizard/See Me Feel Me', the single release from Eve Graham and The New Seekers is the first song in six releases not to make the UK top 20 for the group.

As with the previous single, it is produced by Michael Lloyd and arranged by Tommy Oliver.

PAUL LAYTON: From my understanding, 'Nevertheless', along with some other songs in that same orchestrated ilk, was part of a potential Eve Graham solo project with David Mackay and effectively the song was switched to be branded as a New Seekers single.

SALLY GRAHAM: Eve had a fantastic voice and was great at fronting a group. I'm not so sure if people would have paid money to see Eve perform as a solo artist. In that sense she was no Adele.

EVE GRAHAM: I did become a bit isolated in the group but there again I was always something of a loner. Marty and Paul were great buddies but I guess I lost a chum when Lyn started to go out with Peter Doyle.

For instance, I had friends outside the group when we lived in LA.

I started to feel on top of a merry go round that wasn't ever going to stop. I was still enjoying it but it was intense and our work load didn't show signs of easing off. It was partly through a sense of personal loneliness that I wanted to leave.

You enjoy success if you are enjoying your work. In my view we did get to the point where we wanted to take a break. David Joseph really pushed us. We might have been swearing at him but it was the right thing to do at the time.

We had to keep at it but if you eventually stretch a piece of elastic too much it will snap. That's what I believed happened to us. We kind of burnt out.

NIC CULVERWELL: I think it might have been a mis-step from David Joseph allowing 'Nevertheless' to be released so quickly after the superb 'Pinball Wizard/See Me Feel Me' as in single release terms that was already a huge change of direction for the group.

Whilst it was a superb vocal by Eve Graham, 'Nevertheless' went back to an old fashioned style ballad which was a step backwards to 'Come Softly to Me', which with its 'featuring' aspect only served to confuse the group's fan base.

For instance they could have experienced continued success going in that soft country rock direction with many songs recorded already by the group in that genre, with 'Reap What You Sow' and 'The Further We Reach Out' springing to mind as having good potential for single releases. 'Rusty Hands of Time' would certainly have catapulted the group back into the charts; however, that predominantly featured Peter Doyle and not so much the rest of the group.

There didn't seem to be any clear musical direction with New Seekers single releases at this point in time.

29th April – The New Seekers play The De Montford Hall in Leicester

NIC CULVERWELL: I was able to see The New Seekers' concerts around the country through a combination of juggling part time jobs, my mum's generosity and the fact that in those days tickets were actually not that expensive, in relation to today's prices.

Having seen the group play the Birmingham Odeon the day before, which was in those days the big venue to play in the Midlands in England, I was fortunate to get tickets for Leicester the next day.

Along with a bunch of other fans I was waiting at the stage door to catch a glimpse of the group. My memory is that Marty, Eve and Paul arrived at the venue in a limousine together whilst Lyn and Peter arrived in their own separate one. Lyn got out of the car and went straight into the venue whilst Peter got out and went for a walk around the gardens surrounding the building.

I remember following and introducing myself to him. He made it clear he was going for a walk but invited me to go with him. I started to chat with him but Peter seemed to be in a world of his own and I didn't really understand what he was talking about.

Mind you, I remember thinking Peter Doyle was really cool in doing this with me.

Less than two months away from departing The New Seekers, it is quite possible Peter had a lot on his mind.

30ᵗʰ April – The first broadcast of *The Tomorrow People* on British TV

Produced by Thames Television for ITV, it is seen by many as that network's alternative to the BBC's Dr Who. It is a series that is broadcast in the week fitting into that 'straight after school' slot.

The central premise is that a group of young people 'break out' special powers to become homo superiors ('Tomorrow People'), referred to in the Bowie lyric 'Changes' in a song that appears on his Hunky Dory *album, and face a series of challenges similar to the challenges that appear in* Dr Who.

The final broadcast in the series takes place on the 19ᵗʰ February 1979.

19ᵗʰ May – Marty Kristian is on the front cover of *Look In*

DAVID MACKAY: In The New Seekers Marty became 'the good looking guy with the guitar' who also sang great harmonies.

June 1 – The New Seekers perform 'Goodbye Is Just Another Word' on BBC1

This edition of Top of The Pops *is hosted by the zany Radio One DJ Kenny Everett.*

The single 'Goodbye Is Just Another Word', like previous single 'Nevertheless', reaches the top 40 of the UK charts. It is produced by Michael Lloyd and arranged by Tommy Oliver. Paul Layton co-wrote the flip side 'Me & My Guitar', where he takes on the lead vocals, with Mick Flinn who later on joins The New Seekers.

NIC CULVERWELL: Unlike 'Nevertheless' I felt this WAS a worthy New Seekers release and Eve provides a great vocal.

It is the last hit by the mark two version of The New Seekers and Peter Doyle officially leaves the group afterwards.

NIC CULVERWELL: As a teenager who had just turned 16, I was devastated when I learnt Peter Doyle was leaving the group. I remember reading the headline in *The Wolverhampton Express & Star*.

It was more heartbreaking for me than when the group announced their split in 1974. At that time I couldn't imagine how they could continue as Peter Doyle had such a prominent role in the group.

We were told in the music press Peter left the group because he wanted to go off in his own direction so as fans we had to accept that.

KEITH POTGER: On reflection, in my opinion, I think it was only when Peter started dabbling with drugs that things started to take a turn for the worse. From memory road manager Bill Gavin often had to look after and deal with Peter. I was separate from all of that by this stage as I had ceased to be a tour manager and travel with them.

MARTY KRISTIAN: As time wore on, Peter Doyle was surrounded by some hangers-on as David Joseph's influence lessened.

He became difficult to manage and it affected his performance so consequently from my understanding it was mutually agreed he should leave the band.

PAUL LAYTON: Eve was growing increasingly intolerant of Peter's behaviour. He would always deliver on stage but when it came to rehearsals and turning up on time he was totally unreliable.

KEITH POTGER: It was an indication of Eve's loyalty to the group's image and ethos that she voiced concern over Peter. It was something behind the scenes we had been grappling with and it all came to a head within the group, as opposed to outside the group.

PAUL LAYTON: As Peter was so charismatic, it was dreadfully sad he left, but I believe Eve had a word with our management. It's hard to know but it might have been mutually agreed.

KEITH POTGER: As I recall it the decision was not a mutual one so it was a decision Peter had to grapple with. He was certainly in need of help. We were prepared to help him but there was no way he could continue in the group with the pressure he was bringing on himself, which transferred over to the rest of The New Seekers.

PAUL LAYTON: The decision Peter was leaving the group was presented to me after the fact.

KEITH POTGER: Peter Doyle was a real cornerstone of The New Seekers and his departure really shook the foundations of the group, demonstrating we weren't all pulling in the same direction. David Joseph was pursuing the management of other acts and at that time the American office was becoming more time consuming for him.

I lent Peter Doyle my precious 1965 telecaster and after he left The New Seekers he went to Australia with it. Unfortunately I never got it back.

MICK FLINN: The sound of The New Seekers was never the same after Peter Doyle left.

With many people seeing Peter Doyle as integral, hitting notes others could only dream of with that distinctive vocal delivery, for some their fandom of The New Seekers would have stopped at this point.

The golden era of The New Seekers in evidence with, from left to right, Lyn Paul, Eve Graham, Marty Kristian, Paul Layton and Peter Doyle.

Peter continued to work in the UK until 1981, during which time he released singles, worked on jingles and also provided backing vocals on Lyn Paul's UK hit single 'It Oughta Sell A Million'. He relocated to the US in 1982 where he worked with ex Wings drummer Steve Holly in a group called Regis for five years. In 1991 he returned to Australia.

MICK FLINN: Peter Doyle kept himself to himself but he had a lovely voice. Back in the day he would throw in those high vocal licks that Stevie Wonder did that very few singers could do.

When he went back to Australia, singing in small pub type venues, all the other artists used to go to watch and hear him because he was such a great singer.

They always held him in high esteem, regarding him as one of Australia's greatest singers.

[Note from the author - There is only one Peter Doyle. RIP Peter.]

From June into November – The New Seekers tour North America with Southampton-born singer Larry Oliver replacing Peter Doyle, taking on the stage name Peter Oliver.

DONNA JONES: I thought with Peter leaving it could be the end of the group.

I knew his importance to The New Seekers but, as we had been told ourselves by David Joseph, 'nobody is irreplaceable', and of course the group carried on regardless.

138

KEITH POTGER: To be brutally frank, Peter had become unreliable.

He wasn't unreliable to begin with but things were overwhelming him to such an extent he became that way, so we had to make that change and bring in a replacement.

MICK FLINN: Peter Oliver is a great singer but he wasn't Peter Doyle.

Everyone has their own personality with their vocal delivery. If a key voice in a band leaves it's going to have a different feel and sound without that person being there. It was not the same band anymore.

The New Seekers with Peter Oliver is different from The New Seekers with Peter Doyle.

NIC CULVERWELL: As someone not previously known to the fans, Peter Oliver did an amazing job in filling such big shoes so effortlessly, both appearance wise and musically. In that sense, as a fan I recovered from Peter Doyle leaving instantly. I know other fans felt the same way.

However, a lot of fans didn't feel the same way, and fell by the wayside as their focus with The New Seekers was on Peter Doyle.

The fans that didn't take to Peter Oliver didn't do so as, quite simply, their favourite member of the group was no longer there. For those people, as he was such a crucial part of their idea of The New Seekers, the group could not be their New Seekers. If fans of the group had Eve Graham as their main focus, then those fans may well have fallen by the wayside if she had gone.

Having met Peter Oliver several times, he has always struck me as someone who was 'very much their own person'. He seemed very self assured and aware of his ability as a musician and vocalist. Whilst it must have been a challenge for him, I got the sense he wanted to grasp the opportunity presented to him with The New Seekers, run with it and demonstrate what he was capable of doing.

I never had the impression he saw himself as second best to Peter Doyle. Certainly on stage watching The New Seekers perform he never came across as a replacement figure.

PAUL LAYTON: Whilst Peter Oliver fit in pretty smoothly, first of all it was a matter of him getting to know us all and finding a level with each of us individually. Marty and myself had no problem with him.

Peter Oliver was very motivated. He was a fabulous guitarist and a talented vocalist. He brought a different flavour to the group than Peter

139

Doyle but it was a matter of making some recordings that he could contribute to.

KEITH POTGER: I have no recollection of how we recruited Larry Oliver to take on the role of being Peter's replacement. I would have been busy with other things.

He had good credentials for the group as he was a good singer and guitarist. Larry Oliver, who became Peter Oliver, was a great replacement for Peter Doyle.

29th June - Milkwood release their second single 'I'm A Song Sing Me'

SALLY GRAHAM: We wanted to release original material that Laurie Heath had written. However, the same thing happened with Milkwood as what had happened with The New Seekers, as we got a manager who told us that rather than play Laurie's material we should record 'I'm A Song Sing Me', a Neil Sedaka song.

We thought we were going to be the next America (most famous for the 1972 hit 'Horse With No Name').

Whilst Laurie's song 'Patterson's Brewery' was great it was on the B side and we weren't so keen on that A side.

15th August – New Seekers stablemates Springfield Revival support The Osmonds at The Armory, Legion Field in Birmingham, Alabama

Whilst 'Go Away Little Girl' was a US number one single for 13-year-old Donny Osmond in 1972, 'Puppy Love' is an enormous number one for him in the UK. Donny is portrayed in the media as a rival in the charts to David Cassidy, who also had a solo number one single in 1972.

David is much older than Donny. David also acts in The Partridge Family, *about a make-believe family who are also a pop group, which is a popular show in the UK. However, in 1972 there was also a cartoon series of the Osmonds.*

In this pre Bay City Rollers era, David and Donny are the most popular pin ups for young girls in Britain during this 1972-1973 time period.

Donny belongs to a family of singers and performers. He sings with brothers Alan, Wayne, Merrill and Jay in The Osmonds. In 1972 the group released the terrific theremin driven rock song 'Crazy Horses', written by

Alan, Merrill and Wayne, expressing concerns about the environment, which became a huge hit in the UK. In the summer of 1973 the group released their album The Plan, *expressing their Mormon faith on some of the songs. Although the 1974 release 'Love Me For A Reason' returned the group to the top 10 in the US, in 1973 they were more popular in the UK.*

In September The Osmonds released 'Let Me In', which became another huge hit in the UK, reaching number 2 in the charts and number 4 in the Billboard Contemporary Chart in the US. Nevertheless, Donny Osmond achieved two UK solo number ones in 1973 and even a top 10 hit in the US.

Both The New Seekers and their stablemates Springfield Revival are with The Osmonds on the MGM label in the US.

MICK FLINN: In those days we didn't see it like we were opening for this enormous group The Osmonds. It was presented to us as just a gig.

We travelled round America supporting The Osmonds on a big tour and ended up doing 28 shows in 30 days with them. Unbelievable really when you think of it.

14th September – The New Seekers single 'We've Got To Do It Now' is released

The Cook/Greenaway song is the theme from the 'Keep Britain Tidy' campaign they have become involved in. It is produced by Michael Lloyd and arranged by Tommy Oliver.

The group wearing tops which show the Keep Britain Tidy slogan.
There is a video for the song. Walking in the countryside, the group wear Keep Britain Tidy t-shirts, the boys in yellow and the girls in orange, and before the song begins the other members of the group round on Marty Kristian for dropping some paper, letting him know precisely why it was wrong to do that.
It feels as though musically the kitchen sink is thrown into the production of this song. The single doesn't quite make the top 50 in the UK.

NIC CULVERWELL: I thought it was a fabulous song but it was never going to be successful with, from my understanding, the group halfway round the world in the US, unable to promote it.

KEITH POTGER: Things became fragmented after Peter Doyle left.

GTO films had just started up and I was starting to turn my attention to songwriting away from The New Seekers.

By this time, as The New Seekers were all based in the UK. It must have been strange with how communications were in those days that their manager was based over there in the US.

We were almost becoming like satellites to each other.

NIC CULVERWELL: In my opinion 'We've Got To Do It Now' didn't chart because it wasn't properly promoted!

September – Away from The New Seekers, there is an album release by Marty Kristian, Paul Layton and Peter Oliver
Entitled Peter, Paul & Marty, *as well as interpretations, the release includes two songs by Paul Layton, three songs by Marty Kristian and a Mick Flinn/Paul Layton co-write. It does not chart.*

September 20th – From this date The New Seekers support Liza Minnelli, a performer who is an inspiration to Lyn Paul in particular

PAUL LAYTON: Sadly I lost my father during the tour and Liza, who I already knew a little before I joined The New Seekers, was very supportive over that.

Liza liked to do silly, crazy things. For instance on the plane we travelled on there were waitresses that were topless.

October 30th – The New Seekers appear on Britain's popular children's topical programme *Magpie*, the ITV version of *Blue Peter*
The video for their Keep Britain Tidy campaign song 'We've Got To Do It Now' is shown on this.

November - Forthcoming New Seekers single 'You Won't Find Another Fool Like Me', with a Lyn Paul lead vocal for the first time on a single release, though of course she has taken lead vocals on album tracks, investing huge personality into the delivery, is promoted on BBC1
The group perform it on the 3rd November Lulu *show, the 18th November* Basil Brush Show *and on the 22nd November* Top Of The Pops.

KEITH POTGER: Tony Macaulay, who I'd been songwriting with, co-wrote that song. He had already co written 'Love Grows (Where My Rosemary Goes)', a number one hit for Love Affair, The Foundations hit 'Baby Now That I've Found You' and he went on to produce 'Silver Lady', which was a huge hit for actor David Soul.

NIC CULVERWELL: I was acutely aware, as a fan of the group, that Lyn was being underused, so this was an exciting time for Lyn Paul fans (although she had a fantastic vocal on the *Circles* album with the song 'I Saw The Light').

She really fully demonstrated her vocal ability on this song, as she had done in the 'See Me Feel Me' part of that 'Pinball Wizard' single.

This was Lyn's moment and she passionately grabbed it with both hands. It's a fantastic vocal performance on record by Lyn Paul.

24th November – 'You Won't Find Another Fool Like Me' enters the UK charts
Produced by Tommy Oliver, the single eventually reaches the top of the charts in January 1974.

PAUL LAYTON: 'You Won't Another Fool Like Me' was a change of direction for the group.

The song was written by Macaulay & Stephens, who also came up with our next hit 'I Get A Little Sentimental Over You'. Lyn took the lead vocals on those two songs as they suited her voice.

MARTY KRISTIAN: In my opinion the boat started to rock here and after this song the dynamic in the group became different.

25th November to 20th December – The New Seekers song 'You Won't Find Another Fool Like Me' is promoted on British TV
During this period The New Seekers appear on ITV's The Golden Shot, *the song is played over the chart run down on the 29th November* Top Of The Pops, *and performed live on the 6th December edition with that recording also used on the 20th December programme.*

24th December – Apparently with Eve Graham having given six months' notice, David Joseph tells the group she is to leave The New Seekers

MARTY KRISTIAN: I have a vague recollection there was a meeting but ultimately both Eve and Lyn left, which led to the group folding.

PAUL LAYTON: I don't have any recollection that Eve told us she was going to leave. I heard through our management she was going to leave.

KEITH POTGER: Whilst we used to have conversations, I don't remember any 'formal meetings'. As David Joseph was spending such a lot of time in America such things would have been difficult.

It makes sense it was around this time Eve would have told us she was leaving the group.

25th December – The New Seekers perform 'You Won't Find Another Fool Like Me' on *The Morecambe & Wise Christmas Show*
At the time appearing on this show was hugely prestigious as it was the BBC's flagship show at Christmas with audience figures.

31st December – British Conservative Prime Minister Ted Heath announces the three day week

To reduce electricity consumption, and conserve coal stocks under the Fuel and Electricity (Control) Act 1973, measures come into force at midnight where the commercial use of electricity would be limited to three consecutive days each week.

Television broadcasts were to shut down at 22:30 each evening. The television broadcasting restrictions were introduced on 17 December 1973 but suspended for the Christmas and New Year period. They were finally lifted on 8 February 1974.

It's been a strange year for The New Seekers. With the group reaching peak success the previous year, largely capitalising on the momentum built up by a number one hit and Eurovision success, 1973 has been quite a rocky year as they have lost Peter Doyle yet at the same time gained Peter Oliver.

Whilst there have been high points, perhaps most notably their appearance at the US President's re-election event and the release of 'Pinball Wizard/See Me Feel Me', which has generated much valued US momentum, it has been a year of 'strange releases', for instance 'Nevertheless' and the 'Keep Britain Tidy' campaign, neither of which were well promoted.

On top of that there has been the solo release of 'Crying In The Rain' from Marty Kristian and the 'Peter Paul & Marty' release by the three males of The New Seekers away from the group. Have the management team of David Joseph and Keith Potger taken their hands off the steering wheel at the wrong time?

Without knowing what is happening round the corner, what can fans expect as the momentum is clearly building towards the group experiencing another hit record... surely this will galvanise the group at the right time?

The best selling song in the UK for 1973 was 'Tie A Yellow Ribbon Round The Old Oak Tree' by Dawn featuring Tony Orlando, whilst the song would continue selling well into 1974. 'You Won't Find Another Fool Like Me' was the 42nd best selling single of the year.

146

Chapter 8
1974: Over And Out? - That sad farewell

IN THE UK IN 1974...
*With the general election resulting in a hung parliament and Edward Heath unable to form a coalition with the Liberals, Edward Heath resigns as Prime Minister with Labour leader Harold Wilson coming back into power * Manchester United are relegated to the second division * Alf Ramsey, who guided the England football team to triumph in 1966, is dismissed as their manager * Separate IRA bombings in Guildford and Birmingham pubs kill 26 people * McDonalds open their first restaurant in the UK*

MICK FLINN: With Keith Potger taking less of a hands-on role and David Joseph based now in the US, it did feel that both Springfield Revival and The New Seekers were left in the UK to somewhat manage themselves during 1974.

NIC CULVERWELL: It was announced in the UK daily newspapers in early February that The New Seekers were going to split.
    As a fan I can't say I was overly shocked.

28th February – The New Seekers perform 'I Get A Little Sentimental Over You' on *Top Of The Pops*
The single again features a lead vocal from Lyn and on the 30th March it reaches number 5 in the UK charts. It is produced by Tommy Oliver along with Tony Macauley the co-writer.

NIC CULVERWELL: A lot of New Seekers fans prefer this song to 'Another Fool'. It's more of a group song and it's a lovely song to see performed live.
    Lyn gives it 100% and takes ownership of that song.

MICK FLINN: Those two singles really suited Lyn's voice.

March – The New Seekers album *Together* is released
Somewhat ironically titled, it includes the two 1974 hits, along with 12 other interpretations, which finally includes a New Seekers version of 'Melting Pot' and reaches a UK chart peak of 12. Away from 'I Get A Little Sentimental Over You' Michael Lloyd and Tommy Oliver separately produce tracks on the album.

A FAN'S PERSPECTIVE OF THE ALBUM: The opening 'Friends Medley' was used on tour as a way of the male members of the group putting down their guitars so all of The New Seekers could shake hands with fans in the audience. Eve and Lyn combine effectively on that Mamas & Papas hit 'Dedicated To The One I Love', whilst Lyn does a great job on 'Here, There and Everywhere'. The New Seekers cover of 'Melting Pot' is excellent, putting that politically incorrect lyric to one side. 'The Greatest Song I Ever Heard' is a big favourite with fans. It was recorded two years earlier and had already been released as a US single in July 1973. Marty Kristian feels it's Eve's best vocal performance.

Assisted by the two smash hit singles, the album was a commercial success and for many fans it should have been the group's last album prior to the split.

4ᵗʰ March to 16ᵗʰ May – The New Seekers embark on a UK farewell tour
It begins with a residency at The Talk of The Town in London that lasts until the 23ʳᵈ March, and ends on the 16ᵗʰ May at the Shakespeare Theatre Club in Liverpool. The final two dates, scheduled to take place in Liverpool on the 17ᵗʰ and 18ᵗʰ May, are cancelled. Ironically on the 17ᵗʰ May The New Seekers were presented with The Sun Television Award for Top Pop Act by Neil Sedaka.

PAUL LAYTON: The atmosphere was a bit strained on the tour.

KEITH POTGER: My recollection of the group breaking up is pretty hazy as I was concentrating on other things, mainly my songwriting and GTO publishing, which was doing well in having a presence in the UK.

From my perspective there was a whole cascade of things that happened all at once. It was almost like I was reading about events in the newspaper rather than talking with the individuals themselves. For instance I remember they were looking at new management.

All of these issues combined meant I wasn't sufficiently aware of what was happening with the group.

148

PAUL LAYTON: Both Eve and Lyn seemed keen to call it a day to pursue their own careers.

As long standing members of the group, myself and Marty would have liked to have persuaded them to stay, but there was no way forward with that so we had to accept it.

MARTY KRISTIAN: Paul and myself were disappointed with what happened.

PAUL LAYTON: It was a shame. It seemed we'd got our foot back in the door again, with the different flavour Lyn brought with her lead vocals on those two songs, so we felt there was no need to break up a winning formula.

KEITH POTGER: My management role with The New Seekers ceased when the group broke up in 1974, it was a 'thank you and good night' arrangement effectively.

It's a strange parallel to think that the band functioned for five years, the same length of time The Seekers remained active.

6th April – Abba win the 1974 Eurovision Song Contest, performing 'Waterloo' in Brighton

With their two female, two male line up and vocal harmonising there are some similarities with The New Seekers, although after a slight hiccup in 1975, of course their success, off the back of a distinctive and unique vocal sound with great songs, is remarkable.

27th April – The Bay City Rollers song 'Shang-A-Lang' enters the UK chart at number 35

The song eventually rises to a peak position of number 2 in the charts and sees the beginning of Rollermania, which reaches peak crescendo when their cover of Four Seasons song 'Bye Bye Baby' stays at the top of the UK charts for 6 weeks in 1975.

The single is the first release to feature the vocals of Les McKeown as the previous single was released with lead vocals from Gordon 'Nobby' Clark, even though Les fronts the band when they perform the song on Top Of The Pops.

Commercial success for the group continues on into 1977, but whilst there are single releases after this there are no more hits.

149

7ᵗʰ June – The New Seekers release the single 'Sing Hallelujah'
This time it is a Keith Potger/Tony Macaulay co-write, produced by Tony Macaulay and Tommy Oliver. The single does not chart.

NIC CULVERWELL: It is another Lyn lead vocal but it is not up to the same standard as those previous two hits the group experienced that year.

That song didn't deserve to be a hit in my opinion and by this time the group had gone their separate ways.

28th June - Milkwood release 'What Can I Do To Make You Love Me', their third and final single on Anchor
As with the group's previous two singles, it is not commercially successful.

SALLY GRAHAM: Chris and Laurie went off together to Chicago. After Milkwood ceased to exist under John Brewer's management I signed a solo deal with Anchor records, which was a subsidiary of Warner Brothers, and I became Sally Gee.

Under the moniker Sally Gee, on June 13th 1975 Sally Graham released the single 'Too Much I'm In Love', which is a cover of a Peter Skellern song.

SALLY GRAHAM: It was recorded at Island Studios where I delivered the vocal in a very breathy high-pitched Lynsey de Paul style. I was disappointed it wasn't a hit but it was great fun as I had the musicians who worked behind Cat Stevens playing on that recording. It had great reviews.

CHRIS BARRINGTON: Once the music fizzled out, for a while I ended up going back into acting. Eventually I moved to St Lucia where I discovered my interest in sailing. Sailing became my life.

SALLY GRAHAM: During the period The New Seekers became commercially successful I was very busy refurbishing houses. To me music wasn't a calling, it was just a bit of fun really. It was nice in the reviews for the single release that I was being compared to the singer Minnie Ripperton. After refurbishing several houses I gave up on music altogether. I decided I didn't want to do it anymore.

150

CHRIS BARRINGTON: I found my passion in life was sailing and after leaving The New Seekers I would say I've been lucky enough to have led a very happy life.

SALLY GRAHAM: After the house refurbishments I met my husband and then I went fishing [laughing]. That's me really!

August – The *Farewell Album* is released

Released after The New Seekers ceased to exist, it contained two songs from Peter Oliver and two songs from Marty Kristian. Again the album does not chart. Except for the track 'I Wanna Be The Star Of The Show', which is produced by David Mackay, who also co-wrote the song, the album tracks are produced by Tommy Oliver and Tony Macauley. Each lead vocalist receives a 'featuring' credit.

A FAN'S PERSPECTIVE ON THE ALBUM: It is disappointing there is no group photograph for the cover; instead, positioned in boxes, there are separate photographs of each New Seeker.

As the group has already split up, with this release many fans feel the brand is being milked. The title is odd as the group had already finished.

With the songs on the release it didn't feel as though the group had gone into the studio to record a coherent album. It feels like it was a collection of songs The New Seekers had recorded over the last two years with the record company suggesting that they were stuck on an album. There's no flow to the album.

KEITH POTGER: The legacy of The New Seekers is that they carried forward the name of The Seekers, a name those of us in that group were proud of, which originated in the sixties, into the seventies, and left behind a trail of hits that still resonate in people's hearts today.

NIC CULVERWELL: The New Seekers were a uniquely talented group that had a special sound and left some great music behind them that people still love to hear today.

7th September – The Peter Doyle interview 'The Lost Seeker' appears in *Record Mirror*

It doesn't give much away about the reasons behind his departure from The New Seekers.

Peter makes it clear he stayed in California to make an album but has had a lonely time of it. Apparently Marty treats him extremely nicely, Eve is polite towards him and Paul is cool, although, according to the article, at that time Lyn wasn't getting along with him.

5th December – The last ever episode of Monty Python is broadcast
John Cleese, a key member of the team, has decided he does not want to make any further episodes, though of course 'the comedy group' continues the brand by making a series of films together.

28th December – The fourth Doctor Who, Tom Baker, makes his debut appearance
As well as being the longest serving actor to play the character, until the series gets a reboot in the 21st century, he is the most popular Doctor Who.

The David Essex song 'Gonna Make You A Star' was the best selling song in the UK for 1974, whilst 'You Won't Find Another Fool Like Me' was the 18th best selling single and 'I Get A Little Sentimental Over You' was the 74th best selling single.

Chapter 9
Projects Outside The New Seekers

MPD with Marty, Paul and Danny

PAUL LAYTON: After The New Seekers split, Marty and I decided to develop a three male vocalist project based on a group in Australia called MPD.

After an audition, Kevin Finn joined the two of us and to get the 'D' part of our version of MPD he was rechristened Danny.

MICK FLINN: During the time Marty and Paul had put MPD together with Kevin (AKA Danny) Finn, with Springfield Revival having now finished, I had to give up my flat in London.

As a consequence for a short time I stayed at Marty and Carol Kristian's house in Rickmansworth, Hertfordshire, whilst Marty was rehearsing for MPD.

During that time we occasionally sat around strumming the songs we had on our guitars and when I played him 'The Way That You Do It' he told me it sounded like a hit and that I should put it out.

PAUL LAYTON: As we still had a chunk of New Seekers fans following us we put on a couple of shows and put out some releases.

MARTY KRISTIAN: We weren't going to team up with Peter Oliver as he was romantically entangled with Lyn, who was beginning her solo career. In MPD we set about writing our own songs hoping we might meet with commercial success.

Danny had an even temperament and was very much a 'Mr Nice Guy'. He was also a talented vocalist.

Eve in LA

EVE GRAHAM: On leaving the group I did make some recordings in LA but mainly I went there just to hang out.

Lyn going solo

On the 12th July 1975 the Lyn Paul single 'Oughta Sell A Million', based on that New Seekers advert jingle, with Peter Doyle on backing vocals, reached a peak position of 37 in the UK charts.

After three previous releases without commercial success, Lyn is still the only member of The New Seekers to have had a hit single away from the hits of the group.

Lyn eventually goes on to experience success in the musical Blood Brothers, *where she has been described as 'the definitive Mrs Johnson'.*

Peter Oliver

NIC CULVERWELL: I don't imagine to start with Peter Oliver would have thought of joining The New Seekers as a stepping stone for his solo career although he might have thought of it that way when the group split up.

After The New Seekers split, Peter recorded two singles for RCA and in 1975 joined a version of Paper Lace.

He returned to musicals in 1978 and after that largely performed using his original name of Larry Oliver.

During the whole year of New Seekers inactivity The Bay City Rollers cover of a Frankie Valli & The Four Seasons hit 'Bye Bye Baby' is the best selling song in the UK. I'm afraid that for fans of the group that brief period of New Seekermania had well and truly ended, with Scottish Rollermania sweeping the UK (and many other parts of the world) instead.

154

Chapter 10
The Second Eve Graham Era

1976

PAUL LAYTON: Whilst MPD was active, pressure from The New Seekers' fans made us consider reforming the group. At the time we had written a song 'You Make Me Feel Like A Woman' for a female vocal, with Kathy Ann Rae successfully auditioning to sing that song, and of course she effectively became Lyn's replacement in the next edition of The New   Seekers.

MARTY KRISTIAN: As MPD were not enjoying any commercial success, our manager at the time suggested we reform The New Seekers.

PAUL LAYTON: Eve was asked to consider rejoining The New Seekers. She agreed after listening to the songs we were writing and the demos we'd recorded.

EVE GRAHAM: When I returned from LA the boys said they wanted to reform the group and I came on board as I wasn't doing anything else at the time.

In many ways I returned because I'd enjoyed a two year break from The New Seekers. Before, we had worked so hard we got fed up with what we had to do.

The group having some fun but with another new line up (this time their fourth) with from left to right Paul Layton, Kathy Ann Rae, Marty Kristian, Eve Graham and Danny Finn

16th May – Drury Lane London, The New Seekers perform a reunion concert

Eve, Paul and Marty return with Kevin AKA Danny Finn replacing Peter Oliver and Kathy Ann Rae replacing Lyn Paul in that last 1974 New Seekers line up before the break up.

NIC CULVERWELL: As with Peter Doyle's departure, those fans of the group that had Lyn Paul as their favourite New Seeker would quite possibly have fallen by the wayside at this moment in time.

MARTY KRISTIAN: We were very well received by the fans when we performed the reunion concert and this filled us with optimism for the project.

NIC CULVERWELL: Whilst I was still a fan, by this stage being in my early twenties I was looking to go in a performing direction myself. I attended The Birmingham Theatre School in Birmingham at the time Toyah

Willcox was there, who was a larger than life character who I got to know very well.

By this time the group's support had started to dwindle but as a fan you were nevertheless afforded more time to talk with individual members of The New Seekers backstage before and after performances.

28th August – Released on CBS, 'It's So Nice (To Have You Home)', The New Seekers' comeback single, reaches a peak position of 44 in the UK charts

Produced by Ron Richards and arranged by Tony Hymas, it's a song by Bill Martin and Phil Coulter, who had already written hits for The Bay City Rollers including their big smash 'Shang-A- Lang'.

PAUL LAYTON: It was another incarnation and although we didn't have the same level of commercial success, as with any musical artist, we were still trying to break new ground.

NIC CULVERWELL: Whilst it was great as a fan that The New Seekers were back, unfortunately they had to experience stiff competition from the likes of Abba and (later on especially) The Brotherhood of Man that just hadn't been there in that early 70s period.

They had gone from being the biggest group in the UK within their sector of the record buying market, to potentially becoming also-rans when they reformed.

4th September – 'Dancing Queen' by Abba reaches number 1 in the UK charts

Very disco orientated, it becomes the group's biggest hit and is quite rightly regarded as an iconic pop song.

22nd October – The release of single 'New Rose' by The Damned

It is widely accepted as being the first punk single released in the UK. Although it does not chart, this new genre of music will go overground commercially in 1977.

157

5th November – The New Seekers single 'I Wanna Go Back' is released on CBS

With a lead vocal from Eve, it is another Martin & Coulter song, which they also produce, and it returns The New Seekers to the UK top 30, peaking at number 25.

NIC CULVERWELL: The song had a powerful Eve Graham vocal.

EVE GRAHAM: Although we had that sizeable hit with 'I Wanna Go Back', I didn't feel it was going to be the same as before.

Other groups like ABBA and The Brotherhood of Man had come along with the same format so I felt we were never getting back up to the top again.

The difference between this version and the previous version was that Marty and Paul wanted to write and produce the songs, so in my opinion we were never working at the same level of quality.

It was fine for a while but as far as I was concerned there was no longevity in it.

12th November – The New Seekers album *Together Again* is released on CBS

The album is produced by MPD (Marty, Paul & Danny Ltd).

Although there are song interpretations there are also two Layton, Kristian and Finn co-writes. The album does not chart.

A FAN'S PERSPECTIVE ON THE ALBUM: There was a very measured decision made for the teenage Kathy Ann Rae to initially take on that Lyn Paul look, being her replacement, but of course she had her own personality vocally. The cover is fantastic from the perspective that it very much looks like The New Seekers. 'It's So Nice', their comeback single, wasn't the best choice as their first release. Understandably it feels as though they were a little tentative about their musical direction.

27th December 1976 – The single 'The Way That You Do It' by Pussyfoot enters the Australian charts

It eventually tops the charts in that country and ultimately becomes the second best selling single of 1977 behind 'Don't Cry For Me Argentina'. It is a song written by Mick Flinn and sung by Donna Jones, who are both soon to become members of The New Seekers.

158

MICK FLINN: Just before Springfield Revival finished in 1975 we were looking for that elusive hit single in order to carry on. Geoff Hanlan, our agent, was asking us all if we had any material.

I had been strumming my guitar in my flat and I had this hook ('it's not the way that you do, but you do it to me'), and lines following on from that kept coming into my head. At the time I thought it was a silly little song. However, I recorded it as the last song on my reel of tape.

Geoff went through each of the songs the three of us had. Although I was almost embarrassed to play it, when he heard it, Geoff thought it could be a hit so I recorded a master for it. I changed the arrangement a bit and wrote it in the style of Fox [Noosha Fox's distinctive vocal style is behind the group's smash hit 'S-S-Single Bed', which topped the Australian chart in 1976] but we were discouraged from releasing it as it was felt to be too similar to that group's style, so after that we just did a couple more gigs and Springfield Revival broke up.

In essence we split because we'd literally exhausted every avenue to find that elusive hit for the group. It was very amicable and Ray went over to the US.

On Marty Kristian's suggestion, from his instinct that it had hit potential and thanks to Geoff Hanlan's support, I was able to take ownership of 'The Way That You Do It' recording. I eventually sold it to EMI for £1500, with Nick Mobbs, who signed The Sex Pistols, their A & R guy, where it was released and it became that huge hit in Australia.

Marty suggested Pussyfoot as a group name.

DONNA JONES: In those days record companies were very image conscious. We felt something could be built around that name. Also I was known as someone who found it hard to make a decision and as such I was often pussyfooting around.

The single was banned in the UK. At the time Doreen Davies was Head of Music and Executive Producer at BBC Radio 1 so everything had to be okayed by her. She objected to the name of the group and the name of the song.

MICK FLINN: I knew Molly Meldrum as a Melbourne scenester back in the mid 60s.

At that point in time the TV music show Countdown *was as enormous in Australia as* Top Of The Pops *was in the UK.*

As a presenter for the popular Australian TV show *Countdown*, Molly pre-recorded an interview with me over what I had been doing since

159

The Mixtures. I mentioned 'The Way That You Do It' and I gave him the video for the song. He went off to the US interviewing folk like Elton John and initially mislaid the video. However, on finding it he watched and loved it.

He rang me a while later telling me that on playing a small portion of the video in front of the interview I did with him on *Countdown* the phones went crazy. Molly told me it had to be released in Australia so in the end the masters were flown across from the UK so it could be released there.

And of course the rest is history.....

At the end of the year The New Seekers have reconvened. With punk dawning, rather ironically 'Save Your Kisses For Me' by The Brotherhood of Man is the best selling UK single for 1976.

1977

6th May 1977 – The New Seekers single 'Give Me Love Your Way' is released

Written by Alan Tarney and Trevor Spencer, New Seekers session musicians who had appeared on their albums before the 1974 split, it includes a lead vocal from Marty Kristian and Kathy Ann Rae.

Although highly regarded it is not a hit. It is the group's last US release.

21st July 1977 – The Brotherhood of Man single 'Angelo' is released

Since 1973 this vocal group has had the four person settled line up of males Martin Lee, with the distinctive moustache, and Lee Sheridan, and females Nicky Stevens and Sandra Stevens (no relation), with Sandra the last vocalist to join. Sandra Stevens sang alongside Eve Graham in Manchester based group The Nocturnes but left in 1967 only to be replaced, from Eve's choice, by Lyn Paul.

With the follow up single to the group's 1970 hit 'United We Stand' charting in the UK top 30, since then there had been eleven non charting single releases with the twelfth, 'Save Your Kisses For Me', a huge number one hit and Eurovision Song Contest winner in 1976. Very much of its time, catchy and based around a child-like repetitive hook, with a simple dance routine thrown in for good measure, it is what Chris Barrington would

160

describe as hokey pre mark two New Seekers fare; however, it rebooted The Brotherhood of Man brand.

However, 'Oh Boy', the single preceding 'Angelo', written by Tony Romeo, who also wrote 'I Think I Love You', the huge hit for The Partridge Family, is a catchy pop song that hits the UK top 10 whilst 'Angelo' goes one step further in reaching number 1 in the UK charts.

Written by the male singers in the group and Brotherhood of Man producer Tony Hiller, it is clearly (and unashamedly) based on the Abba template for 'Fernando', albeit more middle of the road. The songwriters understandably have argued they were simply writing 'in the style of the day'.

After 'Angelo' there is 'Figaro' in 1978, which also goes to the top of charts in the UK but with two more hits that year, the last of which fails to breach the UK top 40, they fade from public view a lot faster than The New Seekers.

Out of their next eight single releases only 'Lightning Flash' in 1982 reaches the UK chart, albeit at the lowly placing of number 67.

For a brief period at the back end of the 70s it looks as though The Brotherhood of Man have filled the gap in the market that The New Seekers have left.

28th October 1977 – The album *Never Mind The Bollocks Here's The Sex Pistols* is released on Virgin

A well produced album that contains three top ten singles, the point when the release reaches the top of the UK charts is regarded by many as the time when this punk genre has reached its commercial zenith.

Interestingly, in the year punk broke overground, 'Mull of Kintyre' became a huge hit and is by far the biggest selling single of 1977 in the UK. It's strangely become an almost forgotten song in the legendary Paul McCartney catalogue and today regarded by him, I believe, as a bit of an embarrassment.

1978

20th January 1978 – The Kate Bush single 'Wuthering Heights' is released

With an extraordinary vocal by Kate, who was still at that time a teenager, it went on to top the UK charts for a month. Neither 'middle of the road', 'new wave', 'rock' , 'pop' or 'punk', Kate Bush's music defies categorisation and is distinctly unique to her.

161

18th February 1978 – 'Take A Chance On Me' by Abba reaches number one in the UK charts

From Abba The Album, it is the group's last number one single in the seventies and it could be regarded as their last ever bouncy pop single before they enter their more serious, mature period in the 80s.

16th June 1978 – The film *Grease* is released

Starring John Travolta, following his dancing success with the film Saturday Night Fever, *which re-ignited the career of The Bee Gees, and Olivia Newton John, it becomes a commercial phenomenon garnering solo hits for each of the two central characters. However, the two songs they perform together as a duo, with 'You're The One That I Want' released first of all, followed by 'Summer Nights', become the most successful releases, with each one staying at the top of the UK charts for well over a month (in fact the first release is a number one for nine weeks).*

The reboot of Olivia Newton John's image begins as she shifts away from the middle ground The New Seekers' music is directed towards, appearing as a heavily made up, leather-jacketed 50s moll, in the well known album cover art that advertises the film, based on the character she morphs into at the end of the film.

19th August 1978 – Released on CBS, the New Seekers song 'Anthem (One Day In Every Week)' reaches a UK peak chart position of 21

After the release of 'Give Me Love Your Way', two more singles were released without achieving commercial success; however, 'Anthem (One Day In Every Week)' changed the fortunes of the group.

Quite different from the sound of previous New Seekers hits, you wonder whether it may have influenced vocal group The Flying Pickets, who go on to have an enormous hit with their a capella version of the Yazoo hit 'Only You'. In a varied chart which includes The Commodores at number 1, alongside The Boomtown Rats, X Ray Spex, Sham 69 and Renaissance with their top 10 hit 'Northern Lights', so far it is the group's last UK hit single.

Bizarrely the song is a cover of a Procession song, a 60s Australian band which, like The New Seekers, was managed by David Joseph.

MARTY KRISTIAN: Once again this was a song chosen and produced by David Mackay.

NIC CULVERWELL: It was difficult for the group to perform that song on stage to make it sound like it did on record. However, they made a superb job of it.

It wasn't typical of The New Seekers' sound. It brought new fans on board that wouldn't normally have been interested in the group.

With the group appearing on *Top of The Pops* it was a shame that the week it was rising into the UK top 20 there was a problem with the manufacture of the record as it could have reached a much higher placing.

As the song was falling from the charts unfortunately Danny and Eve announced they were leaving The New Seekers.

September – The New Seekers album *Anthem: One Day In Every Week* is released on CBS

As with previous album Together Again, *it does not experience chart success, although it is difficult to promote with this version of The New Seekers ceasing to exist at around the time of the release as Danny and Eve depart.*

PAUL LAYTON: David Mackay was involved again as a producer. Danny and Eve became romantically involved with each other, leaving the group.

For a while Eve and Danny tour as a duo. Eve does eventually release solo albums and once again David Mackay produces.

18th November 1978 – The single 'Rat Trap' by The Boomtown Rats reaches number 1 in the UK Charts

Commonly accepted as the first new wave number one, the more commercially acceptable term from that time for what the punk genre has now turned into, the group famously rip up posters of John Travolta on Top of The Pops *as songs from the movie* Grease *have dominated the charts that year.*

1978 sees 'Rivers of Babylon/Brown Girl In The Ring' as the best selling UK single, with strong vocals present in a group that on stage consists of three black female singers and the performer Bobby Farrell who, as with the case of the great Maizie Williams who proudly continues to wave the flag of that brand into the 21st century, does not actually appear on the recordings. This should in no way diminish the fantastic lead vocals of Liz Mitchell with Marcia Barrett there too in the mix. Effectively the group is the brainchild of German producer Frank Farian, who provides

163

those bass vocals that Bobby performs. As the 70s end we are most certainly reaching the point of the wholly manufactured band.

The best selling UK song in the final year of the 70s is the ballad 'Bright Eyes' sung by Art Garfunkel and taken from the animated film Watership Down, *demonstrating that commercial success is ultimately always based on a good song being delivered superbly well with a distinctive vocal.*

It is written by the genius songwriter Mike Batt, who was behind the music of The Wombles.

Chapter 11
The Final Chapter Of The New Seekers? - The Brand Continues (1979 to 2010)

After Eve leaves for a second time the group continues, this time focused around longstanding members Marty Kristian and Paul Layton. Brian Engel, a songwriter experienced in the music industry, joins the first post-Eve line up.

BRIAN ENGEL (a member of The New Seekers from 1978 to 1980): The way I saw things was that at the height of their success The New Seekers were salaried performers doing exactly the same as I was.

Previous to joining The New Seekers I had been the lead vocalist and sole songwriter in a soft rock group called Limey that released two albums from 1975 to 1977. Chris White from The Zombies produced the group's second album and Rod Argent, who was also in The Zombies writing hits that included 'She's Not There' and 'Time of the Season', as well as the rock anthem made famous by Kiss, 'God Gave Rock & Roll To You', was also involved as a session man. However, having had experience of near misses in the music business already I began to feel this project was starting to go nowhere.

I was signed to a management company called Evolution, who also dealt with groups that included Renaissance and The New Seekers. Effectively Limey ended when the management company went into liquidation. One of the managers from Evolution approached me, stating that The New Seekers needed a replacement for a singer who had left the group. Initially I baulked at the suggestion but when I was told I would be getting a regular weekly wage I suddenly became more interested in the idea.

Marty and Paul were already good songwriters but what attracted me to the project was they needed some fresh ideas for new songs. They wanted to bring my songwriting skills into the group.

Meeting Marty and Paul, I got on well with them. I felt it would be a good gig as I'd get plenty of work. I guess it did feel a little bit like I was becoming a prostitute but there again, what did it matter? It was a commercial group that paid and to me there was nothing wrong in that. Marty and Paul had set up a company called NS Music yet I could get my songs performed by the group so the package at that time was everything I really wanted. Most of all I wanted to get my songs out there; it wasn't so much about the money.

NIC CULVERWELL: After Eve left the group of course I had continued my own life, although I still saw the group if they were playing at a venue which I could travel to.

However, I do remember there were changes in their line up each time I saw them. For me that didn't matter as I was a deep seated fan of The New Seekers.

By that stage Marty and Paul seemed to be making the decisions, though of course they knew themselves what an individual needed to be the perfect New Seeker. To me there's nothing wrong with taking new people on board as that is how music evolves.

BRIAN ENGEL: The songs were great. For instance 'I'd Like to Teach the World to Sing (In Perfect Harmony)' was a really good single. It wasn't a bad image. Glamorous women and young guys in a group, it was the first time it had happened (before Abba anyway).

My songwriting collaborator Martin Briley was off in America getting legit [he became a touring and session musician with artists that included The Hollies, Olivia Newton John, Cliff Richard, Tom Jones and Donna Summer] so I guess at the time I thought I'd stay for a year and then do something else.

I ended up staying a lot longer than I thought I would.

In our day we all wanted to be pop stars but the thing was we wanted it to be pop stars on our terms. I thought, 'Why fight the music business?' I stopped trying to change the world and decided to join The New Seekers teaching it to sing instead.

To begin with Vivien Banks replaced Eve whilst Brian replaced Kevin (AKA Danny) Finn.

BRIAN ENGEL: Vivien didn't stay for too long, as she didn't fit in. I remember if I did something wrong the boys jokingly told me I would have to get the train back with Vivien.

NIC CULVERWELL: I recall my first show seeing Brian and Vivien with The New Seekers. Vivien seemed absolutely terrified whereas Brian was full of confidence and his experience on stage showed.

I loved Vivien's voice on 'You Needed Me'.

After Vivien leaves, alongside Marty, Paul and Brian, Catriona Walsh and Nicola Kerr join, with Kathy Ann Rae leaving, although she will return again at the end of the Brian Engel period.

166

BRIAN ENGEL: That was my favourite line up. Catriona and Nicola were great singers. That line up worked really well live.

NIC CULVERWELL: The Nicola and Catriona line up was wonderful. Sound wise it was certainly the nearest to that Eve, Lyn, Mary, Paul and Peter Doyle period. Their harmonies worked a treat.

In my opinion, if you listen to the recordings that were made then, this line up was the one closest to the sound of The New Seekers' hits era.

BRIAN ENGEL: Everybody wanted that New Seekers project to be something else. Marty wanted to be someone like Buddy Holly. Paul wanted to be in *Oliver*. Maybe the girls wanted to be models or actresses. The point is that everybody was in the group for their own reasons. Marty and Paul always had someone else pulling the strings and telling them what songs to do.

MARTY KRISTIAN: That line up was very strong vocally.

19th April 1980 – Representing Ireland, Johnny Logan wins the Eurovision song contest singing 'What's Another Year'
The British entry 'Love Enough For Two' by Prima Donna comes third. Prima Donna includes previous New Seeker Danny Finn, who by this time has married Eve Graham. The single just missed out on the UK top 40 when it was released.

The New Seekers attempted to represent the UK again in the Eurovision Song Contest that year with the song 'Tell Me', but it was disqualified shortly before the British heats were televised due to the group already performing the song on TV a year earlier.

NIC CULVERWELL: Of course The New Seekers would have been rehearsing 'Tell Me' but word had got back to the BBC that they had already performed the song on Scottish TV, which had contravened the rules as the entrant songs had to be first time performances.

On the back of that I understand they were promised an album deal by EMI which fell through, from my understanding, with them losing the chance of competing to be the British entrant.

In addition, Mick Flinn and Donna Jones, who will very soon join The New Seekers, were also in the competition to represent the UK. Continuing to use the group name Pussyfoot, they came equal fourth in the competition.

DONNA JONES: At the time, as I was three months pregnant, with the impending British Song For Europe final, hosted by BBC presenter Terry Wogan, around the corner, we didn't know how big I was going to be so we formed an all-girl group for that, with Mick on bass providing backing vocals whilst I was on lead vocals delivering the song.

The song 'I Want To Be Me' was really out there [it has a Lene Lovich, new wave feel] and I guess in many ways was ahead of its time for Eurovision with the format in those days.

MICK FLINN: I co-wrote that song with Mark Stevens, a keyboardist who was a great mate.

October 1980 – Donna Jones, some six years after her departure, follows her friend Lynda Belcher into The New Seekers.

DONNA JONES: Marty and Paul asked me whether I'd like to come into The New Seekers after we had done The Song for Europe with Pussyfoot and I had just become mum of a baby girl.

BRIAN ENGEL: I got on really well with Kathy, Donna and the boys.

DONNA JONES: I was very privileged to be asked to join The New Seekers by Marty and Paul. I loved the group's harmonies and singing their songs.

During the Brian Engel era there are five single releases: 'You Needed Me', a song made famous by Anne Murray, 'Don't Stop The Music' (both on CBS), 'Love Is A Song', 'Tell Me' and 'California Nights' (all on EMI).

BRIAN ENGEL: Those singles could have been more commercially successful but they were never promoted. [Does this sound familiar Nic?]

DONNA JONES: Mick (Flinn) started to tour manage for The New Seekers.

We had a tour of Russia coming up in 1981. With being 8 weeks away from my baby daughter, Marty and Paul checked if I would be okay to do that.

168

MICK FLINN: Not only did I tour manage in Russia, I also stood in as 'Marty Kristian'.

DONNA JONES: With Marty's wife Carol due to give birth in March 1981 he couldn't come for two weeks until their first baby was born (their son Jamie). Mick became Marty for the first two weeks in Russia!
After that Mick was tour manager and helped us with the sound.

18th April 1981 – The Bucks Fizz single 'Making Your Mind Up' reaches number 1 in the charts

Named after a champagne cocktail, the group have recently won the 1981 Eurovision song contest. Taking the Brotherhood of Man template further, their dance routine is most famous for the two male singers ripping off the long dresses of the female singers to reveal they are in fact wearing short skirts.

Without perhaps the vocal skill of The New Seekers, nevertheless with their harmonies, the group become a successful pop group, with UK hits, including two more number ones, running into the mid 80s.

Mick Flinn replaced Brian Engel in The New Seekers during the course of 1981 after standing in for Marty Kristian on that Russian tour.

BRIAN ENGEL: My girlfriend at that time lived in California.
My ideal was to have a design studio in Venice Beach, Florida. I remember sitting in a Bangkok hotel having a cocktail when I broke the news to Marty and Paul that I couldn't do the commute of flying across the world whenever we had a gig anymore.
Mick Flinn took over from me, making it a seamless changeover.

BRIAN ENGEL: Ironically, although the idea was to go over to the US, I ended up meeting my wife in Beckenham soon after my time in The New Seekers ended and there I became a suburban dad for a while.
I gave up the idea of becoming a pop star at that point.

MICK FLINN: When he left, Brian was living around the London area and from my understanding still sang in the pubs/clubs. As well as that I knew he was still writing songs.

169

BRIAN ENGEL: Marty and Paul have become lifelong friends and I really feel part of The New Seekers family.

I thoroughly enjoyed my time in The New Seekers.

MICK FLINN: Brian was a real 'rock 'n' roller'. I didn't feel he was really ever by nature a New Seeker!

DONNA JONES: I know he enjoyed the experience though.

Mick Flinn and Donna Jones join together as a five piece version of The New Seekers with Kathy Rae, who was initially Lyn Paul's replacement, Marty Kristian and Paul Layton.

DONNA JONES: With their last hit back now in 1978, when Mick and myself came into the group, although we loved being in the group, I don't think The New Seekers held the same appeal as they did back in the 70s.

We just battled on to start with.

MICK FLINN: David Joseph was a great manager for The New Seekers before that 1974 split. When we came into the group effectively Marty and Paul ran the show.

I know they had a few managers after David and then from my understanding they drifted away from the idea of having management as they feared that they might get burnt financially.

I think it's fair to say many bands from the 60s and 70s (whether rightly or wrongly) felt management took all the money from them or if they didn't they kept too much for themselves.

DONNA JONES: Marty and Paul were always very fair with us.

With being in Springfield Revival of course we shared the same management company as The New Seekers. We didn't make a lot of money but then it was never about that for me. It was almost like a bonus that I got paid. Singing was something I loved doing irrespective of whether I got paid or not for doing it.

When we were in The New Seekers, to begin with we played on the cabaret circuit, but that got progressively more difficult as venues dwindled over time.

Kathy (now Cathy) Rae finally left The New Seekers in the early 80s.

DONNA JONES: I loved Kathy, she was a beautiful lady...

MICK FLINN: ...And a great singer.

DONNA JONES: Kathy died far too young [in January 2011 aged just 53].

I really admired her and it was a lovely time when she was in the group with us both. I know she left after the Australian tour, I can't be exactly sure why but I think it was for personal reasons.

28th September 1981 – Olivia Newton John releases the single 'Physical'

The reboot of Olivia's image is complete as with short hair and wearing an exercise leotard she goes all sexy in the video. The song reaches the top of the US charts and stays there for an age, appealing to the zeitgeist of this early 80s keep fit generation. The song is middle of the road, but with elements of disco in there it is of its time. In other words, it is a song of the 80s and certainly not a song of the 70s.

NIC CULVERWELL: Around this time variety TV was declining in line with cabaret venues beginning to close.

I'm not sure why this was happening. I guess it was just changing times.

22nd December 1984 – The Black Lace single 'Do The Conga' reaches the top 10

There is another New Seekers connection with Eurovision as current New Seeker Mick Flinn co-wrote this hit for the group, who represented the UK at the 1979 song contest with 'Mary Ann'.

MICK FLINN: It's today's version of 'The Conga', the one they play at all the parties now.

Incidentally the song that preceded 'Do The Conga' is the notorious party favourite 'Agadoo'.

11th March 1985 – Mikhail Gorbachev becomes President of the Soviet Union

Using the slogan of 'Glasnost' he adopts a policy of 'openness and transparency' with the relationship between the Soviet Union on one side and the US/UK on the other side gradually improving.

December 1985 – With a gap of over five years since the last New Seekers release, 'Let The Bells Ring Out Forever' on Tomcat Records is (so far) the final single release by The New Seekers

Featuring the Marty Kristian, Mick Flinn, Donna Jones and Paul Layton line up, the song is a Brian Engel co-write, who was of course a New Seeker for a while, with Dave Hewson, and is published by Hewsongs, whilst the B side is a Marty and Paul co-write that they produced.

BRIAN ENGEL: I wasn't in the band at that time with that single release.

Dave Hewson, who I wrote that song with, had the song idea for a chorus that sounded to me like the basis for a Christmas classic. I still feel today 'Let The Bells Ring Out Forever' has the capacity to be a big Christmas hit record but once again it wasn't properly promoted.

DONNA JONES: I thought that was one of our best new songs.

MICK FLINN: Brian sounded out Marty and Paul, who were keen to do it, so we went in the studio and recorded it.

In 1990 17-year-old Victoria Horn joins the group, becoming Vikki James, with The New Seekers reverting back to the five piece they were before Cathy Rae left

MICK FLINN: As a four piece we missed the other harmonies, it was a lot of work on Donna.

NIC CULVERWELL: When they were a foursome of course they had a different sound, with only Donna on lead vocal and harmony, which wouldn't have been conducive to many fans of the group from the 70s when they were a five piece with two female vocalists.

DONNA JONES: The agent we had at the time thought it would be a good idea in relaunching the brand.

172

MICK FLINN: The New Seekers as a five piece always looks good on stage visually. The agent brought Vikki in and we had a run through with her. We got along with Vikki fine so we thought it would be great.

DONNA JONES: Vikki was great.

A shot taken from a German performance in 1995, showing from left to right Paul Layton, Vikki James, Marty Kristian, Donna Jones and Mick Flinn. There will be another line change into the millennium as Vikki and Marty, who has been a mainstay since the group began, both leave in 2002.

MICK FLINN: Vikki became a very successful songwriter (as for instance in 2003, a song she co-wrote for Enrique Iglesias, featuring Kelis, entitled 'Not in Love' won the Billboard Latin Dance Song of the Year and enjoyed a top ten placing in many sales charts around the world).

In 2002 Vikki James left the group.

MICK FLINN: Vikki was writing a lot of material and wanted to go over to America.

NIC CULVERWELL: After the second departure of Eve Graham, from my understanding the group with the various line ups went into a twenty year phase of constant but not continuous work.

173

I think the friendship that developed amongst Marty Kristian, Mick Flinn, Paul Layton and Donna Jones kept the perfect harmony of The New Seekers going. Without the pressure The New Seekers had when they were successful, with the releases in the 70s and touring internationally or for that matter the fan base, they were simply enjoying their work.

Nic Culverwell comes into The New Seekers story.

MICK FLINN: Just before Marty left the group, we were playing concerts where, with people talking and drinking so much, the audience weren't really noticing what was happening on stage.

At Butlins in Minehead, which was one of those types of concerts, Nic Culverwell, who was a big fan of The New Seekers, came to see us.

NIC CULVERWELL: I was amazed that they'd been playing Butlins and Warners for a number of years.

At Butlins they would have been performing there as part of a 70s themed evening with a variety of acts, some of whom would have been tributes, with each act having 30 minutes performance time.

I was excited to see The New Seekers again. Alongside Marty Kristian and Paul Layton there was also Mick Flinn and Donna Jones, who were by now permanent members of The New Seekers. I remember a lady called Izzy (Isobel Davies) there too, who was standing in for Vikki/Cathy, so they were still a five piece.

They were great but no one was paying the slightest bit of attention to them. I was watching them from a dance floor of spilt beer and I was shocked there was no applause.

I was struck by how unhappy Marty Kristian looked.

MICK FLINN: We invited Nic backstage, where he told us we shouldn't be doing these sorts of gigs.

DONNA JONES: Marty wasn't really enjoying it. We weren't getting great gigs at that time and also we weren't recording.

NIC CULVERWELL: I remember asking Marty Kristian whether he was happy still playing for The New Seekers and he bluntly told me he wasn't. I also had a chat with Paul Layton, Mick Flinn, Donna Jones and Izzy.

I realised at that time they were only getting a few bookings. There wasn't anyone to promote or sell them. As an act I knew they were a commodity that had to be sold. They all seemed a little bit deflated by the circumstances they found themselves in, most especially Marty.

MICK FLINN: Nic stated we merited much better quality concerts and suggested the type of live gigs we should be playing.

The same year as Vikki James departs, after 33 years as a New Seeker, Marty Kristian leaves the group.

MARTY KRISTIAN: After Danny and Eve left, although we had some really talented singers who all contributed wonderfully well, it started to get a bit of a drag for me.

NIC CULVERWELL: A week after my conversation with Marty he left the group. I thought 'Oh my God I was instrumental in Marty Kristian leaving The New Seekers. What have I done!'

MARTY KRISTIAN: I personally felt that I was going nowhere. In the end it wasn't a difficult decision for me to leave the group.

MICK FLINN: After Marty left, responsibility for The New Seekers fell on Paul's shoulders a little bit more. Donna and myself chose to carry on because we enjoyed performing on stage.
    At this point in time we got hold of Mark Hankins and Francine Rees, as well as Roger Walburn (Francine's husband) who came in on guitar.

DONNA JONES: I knew Roger and Francine previously as we played together in a Manchester and Blackpool Mecca house group in 1969/70.

NIC CULVERWELL: Roger, who is no longer with us, was a lovely bloke.

MICK FLINN: I had always liked Francine's voice so I suggested her as a replacement for Vikki to Paul.
    Mark had played in a band with me in the late 70s. He was a great guitarist and singer so he was brought in too.

NIC CULVERWELL: Of course at this point we're talking about people in their fifties, who are mature performers, but like Cathy had done after Lyn left, Francine brought a different, lovely dimension to the group.

Following a New Seekers Convention in 2003, Nic Culverwell is asked to manage The New Seekers, who now consist of Mick Flinn (who takes on a more central role), Donna Jones, Francine Rees, Mark Hankins and Paul Layton, a New Seeker since 1970, with Roger Walburn, who has a key role on guitar

NIC CULVERWELL: I'd organised a fan convention that Mick Flinn, Donna Jones, Francine Rees, Mark Hankins, Paul Layton, Roger Walburn, Cathy Logan (previously Ann Rae), Brian Engel, Marty Kristian and Jill Webster, previous secretary of The New Seekers fan club, attended, alongside a fair few New Seekers fans.

It had been a fabulous event and I became quite friendly with the current members of The New Seekers line up from that.

Over a meal I asked them whether they were content with how things were for them at that time.

MICK FLINN: Clearly we agreed we couldn't manage ourselves and recognised that we needed a spokesman like Nic, who believed in us, to push us.

I asked Nic to manage us.

NIC CULVERWELL: I could have declined that offer but I had a clear vision on what was needed.

I stated that The New Seekers had to put on a proper act so they could go back to playing theatres where the audience listened properly and gave the group the respect the brand deserved.

MICK FLINN: We sat down and discussed the idea of a tour playing to 300 seaters. We knew that we couldn't pull big enough crowds for the bigger venues.

NIC CULVERWELL: I knew what The New Seekers were capable of and the passion was there in me to market them.

MICK FLINN: Nic started to talk with theatres whilst we put together a two hour concert act. It was a combination of New Seekers live material, the hits and new songs.

The group became very, very tight and we reached a very high standard with our sound.

NIC CULVERWELL: It was a challenge talking to people in their 20s managing the theatres about a group they hadn't even heard of who had hits 30 years ago and convincing them to book the group. It certainly wasn't all plain sailing.

However, persistence paid off. I had a lot of theatres who initially refused to book The New Seekers but on the other hand there were a lot who agreed to the group playing at their venue. I kept faith in what I was doing.

MICK FLINN: Nic did a stunning job. He got the press and radio involved. He really made things happen. At the time, when we really needed somebody to do that, he stepped up to the mark.

NIC CULVERWELL: I was proud to have organised a 35 date tour where they were playing pretty much every weekend throughout the year. I feel I brought kudos back for The New Seekers.

We had some nice bookings. I felt it was an achievement for instance to get the group back playing live at The Royal Albert Hall, albeit they were a support act there. The group were invited to play at St James Palace for Charles and Camilla's Christmas party. As well as that The New Seekers performed at two Buckingham Palace garden parties.

Over a five year period the group played 250 dates and that was really exciting and rewarding for all involved.

27th June 2007 – The New Seekers play at The Banks Stadium in Walsall

This is 'a sort of homecoming' for their Bloxwich-born manager Nic Culverwell

NIC CULVERWELL: Walsall is my home town.

A huge part of being successful as a manager is knowing how to say the right thing at the right time, along with being skilled at marketing. When I was pitching The New Seekers to the local newspaper, I had to write some copy that was topical, hence the idea of including some lines about watching Walsall FC play with my grandfather.

He is successful with this as it leads to an article on the concert in Wolverhampton's The Express & Star.

NIC CULVERWELL: I always loved music and was never actually much of a football fan. However, it was lovely that they played at that cabaret venue within Walsall football club in my hometown!

With the tour progressing well, thoughts turn to developing material for a new album.

MICK FLINN: In thinking about a new album we recorded around 20 new songs.

Nic spoke with Brian Berg, who was president of Universal at the time, who was very encouraging. However, ultimately he supported the idea of a New Seekers greatest hits album as opposed to an album of new material.

NIC CULVERWELL: To be fair, Universal were very committed to a new release.

There is a 2009 CD release called It's Been Too Long...The New Seekers: Greatest Hits & More.

MICK FLINN: We wanted to include some new material so the name of the album had 'Greatest Hits & More' in the title.

There are five new tracks from the current line up and a song from Marty Kristian, with all the other tracks coming from the era of The New Seekers up to and including 1978. By now Marty Kristian and Paul Layton own The New Seekers brand.

MICK FLINN: We did a lot of TV, including BBC Breakfast, but we would have preferred to have released an album that contained our own new material.

NIC CULVERWELL: I attended numerous meetings where we discussed subjects such as the artwork for the release. It was quite a long process but ultimately it was very successful.

The release brings The New Seekers another top 20 hit, reaching number 17 in the UK charts!
Although Mick Finn was not part of The New Seekers during the era of their hit singles, he was nevertheless a member of The New Seekers for almost thirty years.

MICK FLINN: I have really loved being part of The New Seekers.

I enjoyed the camaraderie of the group. I loved working with Paul, Marty, Donna, Francine, Roger and Mark. We had some fun, saw a lot of the world and they were great times.

178

The New Seekers' songs were great to sing. I particularly enjoyed the feel of 'Never Ending Song Of Love' as people really got behind it when we played it live. The New Seekers' version of 'Blackberry Way' is great to do too, as it's such a good song.

The New Seekers, with Paul Layton at the helm, have not been active since 2010.

NIC CULVERWELL: In 2010 The New Seekers took part in a Belgium 'hits of the decade' show for a promoter and afterwards just concentrated on a few private shows.

We could have continued but The New Seekers had played every theatre that was going to take them once (if not twice). If you carry on playing the same venues too long you run the risk of losing your audience as the show becomes diluted.

I still get offers coming in to me asking The New Seekers to perform. To me The New Seekers have never said they will never again do any more shows. However, there would have to be a viable good reason to accept a booking, considering a backline and sound team would have to be put together, as this is costly and challenging logistically.

Whilst Nic is diplomatic in not ruling out a return of The New Seekers I fear Paul Layton, who many see as now being the custodian of the brand, is not as positive.

PAUL LAYTON: Of course The New Seekers have been a huge part of my life.

Although the group hasn't been active since 2010 and no announcement has been made that they have broken up, I instinctively feel The New Seekers should be left to die a natural death!

For you, having just read the story, is there just one version of The New Seekers or, with twenty people performing under the brand, have there been many? In fact, could there even be another new version waiting for us someday round the corner?

However, for the fans of The New Seekers it would seem that with Paul's comments we will just be left with the memories of the feelings we experienced when we heard the group singing in perfect harmony!

Afterword by Paul Layton

My time with The New Seekers has been a great experience. I have made many friends, including ones that have been life-long, who have supported and educated me in many ways.

I was able to participate in and experience things that would have, most probably, not have come my way without being within The New Seekers and to travel and visit places that have enriched my life.

I have loved entertaining people and seeing the joy on their faces, especially the fans that stuck with us through the changing line-ups of the group, some of who remain friends today.

Paul Layton, March 2022

Selected Discography

Whilst readers can look back within the text for more detail on the UK releases, I decided to just emphasise the scale of The New Seekers' commercial success in this section.

Charting Albums

THE UK:

September 1971 *New Colours* peak chart position of 40

March 1972 *We'd Like To Teach The World To Sing* peaks at 2

June 1972 *Never Ending Song of Love* peaks at 35

September 1972 *Circles* peaks at 23

March 1973 *Now* peaks at 47

March 1974 *Together* peaks at 12

July 2009 *It's Been Too Long - Greatest Hits & More* peaks at 17

THE US:

May 1971 *Beautiful People* peaks at 136 in the Billboard charts

December 1971 *We'd Like To Teach The World To Sing* peaks at 37

September 1972 *Circles* peaks at 166

March 1973 *Now* peaks at 190

Charting Singles

THE UK:

July 1970 'Look What They've Done To My Song Ma' peaks at 44

June 1971 'Never Ending Song Of Love' peaks at 2

October 1971 'Good Old Fashioned Music' peaks at 53

December 1971 'I'd Like To Teach The World To Sing (In Perfect Harmony)' reaches number 1

March 1972 'Beg, Steal Or Borrow' peaks at 2

June 1972 'Circles' peaks at 4

November 1972 'Come Softly To Me' peaks at 20

February 1973 'Pinball Wizard/See Me Feel Me' peaks at 16

March 1973 'Nevertheless' peaks at 34

June 1973 'Goodbye Is Just Another Word' peaks at 36

September 1973 'We've Got To Do It Now' peaks at 53

November 1973 'You Won't Find Another Fool Like Me' reaches number 1

March 1974 'I Get a Little Sentimental Over You' peaks at 5

June 1976 'It's So Nice (To Have You Home)' peaks at 44

November 1976 'I Wanna Go Back' peaks at 25

June 1978 'Anthem (One Day In Every Week)' peaks at 21

THE US:

June 1970 'What Have They Done To My Song Ma' peaks at 14

October 1970 'Beautiful People'/'When There's No Love Left' peaks at 67

March 1971 'Nickel Song' peaks at 81

December 1971 'I'd Like To Teach The World To Sing (In Perfect Harmony)' peaks at 7

March 1972 'Beg, Steal Or Borrow' peaks at 81

June 1972 'Circles' peaks at 87

September 1972 'Dance Dance Dance' peaks at 84

November 1972 'Come Softly To Me' peaks at 95

February 1973 'Pinball Wizard/See Me Feel Me' peaks at 29

AUSTRALIA:

June 1970 'Look What They've Done To My Song Ma' peaks at 3

March 1971 'Nickel Song' peaks at 67

June 1971 'Never Ending Song Of Love' peaks at 25

December 1971 'I'd Like To Teach The World To Sing (In Perfect Harmony)' peaks at 7

March 1972 'Beg, Steal Or Borrow' peaks at 36

June 1972 'Circles' peaks at 20

November 1972 'Come Softly To Me' peaks at 73

February 1973 'Pinball Wizard/See Me Feel Me' peaks at 16

March 1973 'Nevertheless' peaks at 96

November 1973 'You Won't find Another Fool Like Me' peaks at 5

March 1974 'I Get A Little Sentimental Over You' peaks at 12

June 1976 'It So Nice To Have You Home' peaks at 72

Note: 'Never Ending Song Of Love' reached number one in Ireland, where 'I'd Like To Teach The World To Sing' and 'You Won't Find Another Fool Like Me' also became number one hits.

Epilogue

And so, for me, the story of The New Seekers is the story of a project established in the UK by two Australians, Keith Potger and David Joseph, to continue the musical legacy of The Seekers but in a different format, and with two female singers central to the new sound of these 'new' Seekers.

As the group were unable to gel first of all, with 60% of their personnel uncomfortable with the direction the project was taking, the brand was relaunched in 1970 with three new singers.

Through a combination of that unique perfect harmony, skill and the team work of many people behind the scenes, the group started to experience significant success in the UK of 1971, after starting to show signs of promise the year before in the US.

1972 was the year of The New Seekers but the momentum slowed in 1973 with the management perhaps taking their foot off the gas, and as Peter Doyle was replaced. With renewed commercial success in 1974, The New Seekers split that year but reformed in 1976. Another new line up brought some success but times had changed in the era of The Brotherhood of Man, Boney M and Abba.

After Eve Graham's second departure, as you have read, the group continued on with Paul Layton as the mainstay throughout the time they remained active, as Marty left early in the new millennium with Donna Jones and Mick Flinn important members from the 80s until their last performance in 2010.

The New Seekers have certainly left their mark in pop music history...

My thanks go to Nic Culverwell, who is still the manager of The New Seekers, for helping me with this project every step of the way!

As well as this, it was great having Marty and Paul so openly supportive.

On top of that, Eve's emails were hugely motivating, as was my conversation with musical legend Keith Potger, with both individuals kindly giving me so much of their time.

Carrying on with that theme, my goodness, Mick Flinn and Donna Jones were HUGELY giving of their time. Thanks guys and I owe you one Mick.

My conversations with Chris Barrington and Brian Engel were hugely entertaining. Both brilliant people to sit next to at a dinner party or dare I say it 'down the pub'.

Appropriately it was my conversation with David Mackay that started things off, facilitated by the tremendous Australia based publicist Chris Maric, who told me 'I think my connection with David might interest you Neil.' Just a little Chris. LOL as they say in this internet era...

And last but not least my long, enjoyable conversation with Sally Graham, who has a wicked sense of humour, was an unexpected but joyous pleasure.

I hope you have enjoyed reading *Perfect Harmony: The New Seekers Story*. In many ways it was a fable of the sadly long gone powerful pre-internet television era that I grew up embracing. However there's nothing more certain as change itself... we must all adapt.

Neil Saint, author